THE WORKS OF LI-PO

THE CHINESE POET

DONE INTO ENGLISH VERSE BY SHIGEYOSHI OBATA

WITH AN INTRODUCTION AND BIOGRAPHICAL
AND CRITICAL MATTER TRANSLATED FROM THE CHINESE

A Digireads.com Book
Digireads.com Publishing

The Works of Li Po
By Li Po
Translated by Shigeyoshi Obata
ISBN 10: 1-4209-4296-4
ISBN 13: 978-1-4209-4296-5

Please visit *www.digireads.com*

PREFACE

This is the first attempt ever made to deal with any single Chinese poet exclusively in one book for the purpose of introducing him to the English-speaking world.

Li Po has been the best-known Chinese poet in the Orient for the last one thousand years or more. In America his name has only recently been made familiar to the poetry public through the translation of his poems by eminent contemporary poets. But as the Bibliography at the end of the present volume indicates, Li Po—variously designated as Le Pih, Ly Pé, Li Taipé, Li Tai-po, *et cet.*—has been known more or less to Europe during the past century. A prominent place is accorded the poet in all the French and German anthologies of Chinese poems, which have appeared from time to time. He is included among the *Portraits des Célèbres Chinois* in Amiot's *Mémoires* (1776-97), while Pavie's *Contes Chinois* (1839) has a *nouvelle* of his life. Excellent studies and translations have been made by two German scholars, Florenz and Bernhardi, in their monographs on the poet.

In the English language, there is Mr. Edkins' paper "On Li Tai-po," which was read before the Peking Oriental Society in 1888 and was published in that Society's Journal in 1890. Mr. Edkins was perhaps the first Englishman to pay special attention to our poet, though his translations are trite and barren. Professor Giles' *Chinese Poetry in English Verse* and *History of Chinese Literature* came out respectively in 1898 and 1901. While his dexterous renderings of Li Po and other poets have since been generally accepted as standard English versions, they fail to create an appetite for more of their kind owing probably to the professor's glib and homely Victorian rhetoric which is not to the taste of the present day. Mr. Cranmer-Byng is elegant, but somewhat prolix. His two books, *A Lute of Jade* and *A Feast of Lanterns*, have many gorgeous lines, suffused, I fear, with a little too much of Mr. Cranmer-Byng's own impassioned poetry. These three men belong to the old school of translators, who usually employ rhyme and stanzaic forms.

Then, in 1915, Mr. Ezra Pound entered the field with his *Cathay*, a slender volume of a dozen or more poems mostly of Li Po, "translated from the notes of the late Professor Fenollosa and the decipherings of Professors Mori and Ariga." In spite of its small size and its extravagant errors the book possesses abundant color, freshness and poignancy, and is in spirit and style the first product of what may be called the new school of free-verse translators, who are much in evidence nowadays. I confess that it was Mr. Pound's little book that exasperated me and at the same time awakened me to the realization of new possibilities so that I began seriously to do translations myself. Mr. Waley omits Li Po from his first book, but includes in his *More Translations* a few specimens from a group of poems that he published in the *Asiatic Review*, in which he avers that he does not regard Li Po so highly as others do. On the other hand, Miss Lowell devotes her recent delightful volume, *Fir-Flower Tablets*, largely to our poet, with a selection of eighty-five poems by him. Mr. Bynner's translation of what he calls *Three Hundred Pearls of Tang Poetry*, has been announced for early publication, in which Li Po will be represented by some twenty-five poems.

Now to the Western literary world, generally speaking, much of Chinese poetry remains still an uncharted sea for adventure. The romantic explorer who comes home from it may tell any tale to the eager and credulous folk. Not that yarns are wilfully fabricated, but on these strange vasty waters, dimly illumined with knowledge, one may see things that are not there and may not see things that are really there. Such is certainly the case with Li Po. For instance, Mr. Edkins speaks of a poem (No. 72) which he entitles "A Japanese Lost at Sea," as being "unknown in China" but having been preserved by the Japanese. He adds with the pride of a discoverer that the poem was given him by Japanese in 1888, whereas as a matter of fact the same poem has for these centuries had a place in any Chinese edition of Li Po's complete works. Take another example. Due to the devious and extremely hazardous nature of his method of translation, Mr. Pound gathers two different poems of Li Po into one, incorporating the title of the second piece in the body of his baffling conglomeration. Even Mr. Waley registers his fallibility by a curiously elaborate piece of mistranslation in the *Asiatic Review*. Speaking of Li Po's death, he quotes from Li Yang-ping's *Preface* a passage, rendering it as follows:

> When he was about to hang up his cap (a euphemism for dying), Li
> Po was worried...

which should read, to follow Mr. Waley's manner,

> When I was about to hang up my cap (a euphemism for resigning
> from office), Li Po was sick...

"Kua Kuan," a quite common Chinese phrase, meaning to hang one's cap, that is, one's official cap, is never used as a conceit for dying. In her Introduction to *Fir-Flower Tablets*, Mrs. Ayscough is right in rejecting the tempting morsel of legend about Li Po's drowning, which has been accepted by Professor Giles and others. But on the same page she makes a misstatement to the effect that Li Po after his return from exile went to "live with his friend and disciple, Lu Yang-ping, in the mountains near Kiu Kiang." The fact is Li Yang-ping (not Lu Yang-ping) was then magistrate of Tang-tu, the present city of Tai-ping in the province of Anhwei, at a considerable distance from the Lu Mountains, which are in Hunan. Nor does she seem to be conversant with the notorious bit of China's literary history regarding the "Eight Immortals of the Winecup." They acquired their enviable fame in the taverns of Chang-an during Li Po's sojourn in that metropolis. Tu Fu's celebrated poem (No. 125) will serve as an evidence. The group never lived in the mountains together as Mrs. Ayscough makes out. Again she blunders glaringly and inexcusably in writing, "China's three greatest poets, Li Tai-po, Tu Fu, and Po Chu-i all lived during his (Ming Huang's) long reign of forty-five years," for elsewhere in her own book the years of these poets are correctly given to be respectively, A. D. 701-762, 712-770 and 772-846.

By citing these few obvious errors committed by zealous scholars and daring poets, I do not mean to discredit their brilliant achievements, which I fully appreciate, and to which I am heavily indebted in the execution of my work. Only I feel it my duty to indicate to my reader the still very imperfect state of what is accessible to him in the way of a Li Po literature in English. And conscious of my own failings, I offer him my book in all humility although I have profited by the contributions of my predecessors, and although I feel that in the limited scope I have chosen, my work is generally adequate.

I am a Japanese. I pretend to no erudition in Chinese literature. But I have been all my life a student and lover of Chinese poetry, or as much of it as I can read. In my boyhood I learned some shorter pieces of Li Po by heart. And during these past years of my study and travel in America I have always carried with me a small edition of his works. These translations were made at intervals, over half of them having been finished before the spring of 1916. It is more than a year since the entire collection was completed and I began to look for a publisher. A few of the poems were published in the *Wisconsin Literary Magazine*, a student publication at the University of Wisconsin where I did my graduate work in English during 1917-1918. One poem (No. 9) was printed by a friendly editor in 1919 in the now defunct *Art and Life*. All the rest is presented to the public for the first time.

For the historical and biographical matter in the *Introduction* I drew only on the most reliable Chinese sources such as the writings of the poet himself and his contemporaries and the two *Books of Tang*, while I referred constantly to the works of European historians and translators. As to the poems themselves, they represent only a little more than one-tenth of the works of Li Po preserved in the standard Chinese edition, but I have tried to make the selection as varied and representative as possible and included, consequently, a number of popular pieces which have been translated by more than one hand. I have honestly tried my best to follow the original poems closely and to preserve the peculiar emotional color of each poem, waiting for the moment when I was in the right mood to take up a particular piece. For the elucidation of the difficult passages I depended largely on Japanese and Chinese commentaries, and consulted freely, wherever possible, existing European translations; and I had also the assistance of my Chinese friends. But I wish to have my reader understand that many of my versions are far from being literal. A literal translation would often leave a Chinese poem unintelligible unless supplied with a great amount of exegesis, and I did not wish to empty all the rich content of the original into footnotes. I have amplified or paraphrased on many occasions. I have omitted unimportant words here and there. I have discarded, or translated, a number of proper names because, some way or other, Chinese syllables refuse to sing in company with English words. I have dropped all the phonetic marks, which indicate some tonal peculiarities in certain words like T'ang yün, fêng, etc., but which serve only to mystify a non-initiate like myself or my reader. But after all these and other things I have done, I am inclined to believe that my renderings are often simpler and more exact than other extant versions, which I have studied and which I have listed at the end of the book.

In conclusion, I acknowledge my heavy obligations to all my European and American precursors in the field and to my many personal friends who have aided me in various ways during these years of protracted toil. I mention specially my Chinese friend, Mr. Yulan Fung, who went over the entire manuscript and furnished me with valuable criticism and corrections, and also Mr. Lo and Mr. Yang who did for me the Chinese titles of the poems, which appear at the margins of the succeeding pages. Finally my deepest gratitude is due to my old friend, Arthur Harcourt Mountain, without whose enthusiastic interest and frequent companionship and collaboration this book might have never been brought to completion.

SHIGEYOSHI OBATA.

February 3rd, 1922.

CONTENTS

8

POEMS BY LI PO

INTRODUCTION

I

At the early dawn of medieval Europe China had reached the noontide of her civilization. Indeed, the three hundred years of the Tang dynasty beginning with the seventh century witnessed a most brilliant era of culture and refinement, unsurpassed in all the annals of the Middle Kingdom. And the greatest of all the artistic attainments of this period was in literature, and particularly in poetry. There were no dramatists; no romancers; but only poets—and poets there were galore.

"In this age," remarks a native critic, "whoever was a man, was a poet." And this is not satire. The "Anthology of the Tang Dynasty" consists of nine hundred Books and contains more than forty-eight thousand nine hundred poems by no less than two thousand three hundred poets. Moreover, since this collection was compiled as late as the eighteenth century by order of a Manchu emperor, it represents only a meager crop from a field that had suffered the ruthless ravages of time for fully a thousand years. Imagine, then, the vast efflorescence of what must have been veritably a tropic jungle of poesy!

Now a person may consider it no distinction to be counted one among these poets when the list is so large; but to be picked out as the greatest of them all—as the leader of this colossal army of immortals, is certainly a singular distinction and honor. And this honor falls to Li Po. He, by almost unanimous consent, is regarded as the greatest poet under the Tangs, and of China of all times. "He is the lofty peak of Tai," proclaims an admirer, "towering above ten thousand mountains and hills; he is the sun in whose presence a million stars of heaven lose their scintillating splendor."

Before attempting to follow the poet's career in detail, let us take a glance at China as it was under the Tang dynasty, especially under the famous emperor Hsuan Tsung, who was one time patron to Li Po, and whose long and illustrious reign, ending with his tragic fall, marks the golden age of Chinese poetry.

II

The Tangs came to power in the early decades of the seventh century when Mahomet was just starting out on his first campaigns. Tai Tsung, the second emperor of the dynasty, in the twenty-three years of his reign (627-650) consolidated the hostile sections of the country and laid a firm foundation for his empire, which he greatly expanded by conquering Tibet and subduing the Tartar tribes of the Mongolian desert. Wu Hu—an empress (684-704)—has been much maligned for usurping the male prerogative of sovereignty; but she was undoubtedly one of China's ablest rulers and did more than uphold the prestige of her land during the last quarter of the century. Then followed shortly Hsuan Tsung, who ascended the dragon throne in 713 and ruled for forty-two years.

It was an age of great political power for China. Her suzeraignty extended from Siberia to the Himalaya mountain range, and from Korea to the Caspian Sea. Tributes were paid by India and Tonkin. The Caliphs of Medina sent precious stones, horses, and spice. From the Japanese capital, Nara, came envoys and students at frequent intervals, while once, in 643, from far Greece Emperor Theodosius despatched a mission to the court of Cathay.

It was an age of prosperity. The fertile valleys of the Yellow River and the Yangtze-kiang were turned into fields of rice, barley and waving corn, amid gleaming streams and lakes. Peace reigned in China proper—the vast domain that had once been torn up and made desolate by internecine wars during the four centuries of the *Three Kingdoms* and the *Six Dynasties*. Even in the remotest rural district, the *wine-pennant*, a tavern sign, was seen flying on the roadside, denoting the presence of tranquility and good cheer, while large cities like Lo-yang (i.e. Honan-fu, Honan) and Chin-ling (i.e. Nanking, Kiansu) flourished immensely with increasing trade and travel.

Chang-an, the present city of Hsian-fu in Shensi, was the capital and the wonder of the age. The city was never so rich, splendid, and spendthrift. "See ye," proudly sings a poet, "the splendor of the imperial abode, and know the majesty of the Son of Heaven!" Beside the main castle with its nine-fold gates, there were thirty-six imperial palaces that reared over the city their resplendent towers and pillars of gold, while innumerable mansions and villas of noblemen vied with one another in magnificence. By day the broad avenues were thronged with motley crowds of townfolk, gallants on horseback, and mandarin cars drawn by yokes of black oxen. And there were countless houses of pleasure, which opened their doors by night, and which abounded in song, dance, wine and pretty women with faces like the moon.

It was also an age of religious proselytism. Buddhism had been in China for centuries before the Tang dynasty, and the country was dotted with monasteries and pagodas. It was in the reign of Tai Tsung that Yuen Tsang, a Buddhist priest, made his famous pilgrimage to India and brought back several hundred volumes of Sanscrit sutras. While Confucianism remained ostensibly the guiding principle of state and social morality, Taoism had gathered a rich incrustation of mythology and superstition and was fast winning a following of both the court and the common people. Laotzu, the founder of the religion, was claimed by the reigning dynasty as its remote progenitor and was honored with an imperial title. In 636 the Nestorian missionaries were allowed to settle in Chang-an and erect their church. They were followed by Zoroastrians, and even Saracens who entered the Chinese capital with their sword in sheath.

Thus Chang-an became not only the center of religious proselytism, but also a great cosmopolitan city where Syrians, Arabs, Persians, Tartars, Tibetans, Koreans, Japanese and Tonkinese and other peoples of widely divergent races and faiths lived side by side, presenting a remarkable contrast to the ferocious religious and racial strife then prevailing in Europe. Again, in Chang-an there were colleges of various grades, beside special institutes for calligraphy, arithmetic and music. Astronomy was encouraged by Tai Tsung, who also filled the imperial library with more than two hundred thousand books. Hsuan Tsung saw to it that there was a school in every village in the fifteen provinces of his empire.

Hsuan Tsung himself was regarded as a perfect prince, wise and valiant, a sportsman accomplished in all knightly exercises and a master of all elegant arts. Being a musician, he established in his palace an operatic school, called the "Pear Garden," at which both male and female actors were trained, and in which historians find the prototype of the modern Chinese drama. The emperor surrounded himself with a brilliant court of poets, artists, and beautiful women. Odes were offered him by Li Po and Tu Fu; Li Kuei-nien sang at his bidding, while Yang Kuei-fei, the loveliest of the three thousand palace ladies, ever accompanied his palanquin. Although in his latter years he indulged in all sorts of extravagant revelry, he was never vulgar. It is fitting that he is still remembered by the name of *Ming Huang*—the "Illustrious Sovereign."

But in order to complete the picture of this era there is a darker side, which really brought into full play the spiritual energies of the Chinese race. Within, the court, from the very beginning of the dynasty, was upset more than once by the bloody intrigues of princes and princesses who coveted the imperial crown. Without, China had her Vandals and Goths and Franks, to whom her wealth and splendor offered irresistible temptation to pillage. The border warfare never ceased, and not without many a serious reverse for the imperial forces, which made forays in retaliation, often far into the hostile territories, losing their men by thousands. Tai Tsung's Korean expedition was nothing but a gigantic fiasco, and the conquest of that peninsula was completed by generals of the Empress, Wu Hu. But in her reign the Kitans, a redoubtable foe, appeared on the northern border. In the west the restive and warlike Tibetans could not be wholly pacified by political marriages, in which the imperial princesses were bestowed on the barbarian chieftains from time to time. The armies of Hsuan Tsung were most unfortunate. In 751 thirty thousand men perished in the desert of Gobi; while in the campaigns in Yunnan against the southern barbarians the Chinese lost, it is said, two hundred thousand men. Finally came the rebellion of An Lu-shan, which like a storm swept the mid-imperial plains, drenched them in blood, and left the empire tottering on the brink of ruin.

An Lu-shan was a soldier of the Kitan race, who distinguished himself in fighting against his own tribes, and who won the favor of Yang Kuei-fei and the confidence of Hsuan Tsung. His promotion was rapid. He was ennobled as a duke, and made the governor of the border provinces of the north, where he held under command the best armies of the empire and nursed an inordinate ambition, biding his time. Meanwhile at the court, the blind love of Hsuan Tsung for Yang Kuei-fei was corrupting the government. Her brother Yang Kuo-chung was appointed prime-minister, while eunuchs held high offices of state. At last in the spring of 755, An Lu-shan, under the pretext of ridding the court of Yang Kuo-chung, raised the standard of rebellion. He quickly captured the city of Lo-yang, occupied the entire territory north of the Yellow River, comprising the provinces of Shansi and Chili, and was soon marching eastward on Chang-an. He had proclaimed himself the Emperor of the Great Yen dynasty.

"Is it possible!" exclaimed Hsuan Tsung, now an aged monarch, in amazement at the ingratitude of his vassal and at the impending catastrophe. The defense at the Pass of Tung Kwan collapsed. The emperor was forced to flee from the capital one rainy morning, with his favorite mistress and a handful of his faithful servants. The soldiers escorting Hsuan Tsung blamed Yang Kuo-chung for the disaster, and he and all his kin were massacred. Yang Kuei-fei herself did not escape. She was ruthlessly snatched from the arms of her imperial lover, and was strangled and buried on the roadside without ceremony. The emperor abdicated in favor of his son, and proceeded mournfully to Ssuchuan, the land of Shuh.

The new emperor, Su Tsung, mustered a strong army under General Kuo Tsu-i to oppose the foes. Confusion was added by the revolt of Prince Ling, the sixteenth son of Hsuan Tsung, who challenged the authority of his brother from his stronghold in the southern provinces, though this uprising was promptly suppressed. An Lu-shan was driven from Chang-an in 757, and was shortly murdered by his own son, who was in turn killed by An Lu-shan's general, Shi Ssu-ming, another Kitan Tartar, who assumed the imperial title and retained the northern provinces in his iron grip. But Shi Ssu-ming himself was soon assassinated by his son, and the rebellion came finally to an end in 762.

We need not follow the history longer. In that very year the former emperor, Hsuan Tsung, who had returned from exile to a lonely palace in Chang-an, died, broken-hearted.

Such was the era. It had, on the one hand, internal peace, prosperity, cosmopolitan culture, profuse hospitalities and literary patronage; on the other, distant wars, court intrigues and, finally, the national catastrophe with its tragic drama of stupendous magnitude, that brought forth Li Po and his race of poets, kindled their imagination, and touched their heart-strings to immortal song.

III

The ancestry of Li Po is traced back through the obscurity of many generations to Li Kao of the fifth century, who ruled the Liang State, or the western portion of what is now the province of Kansu. The family dwelt in exile for a period in the Mongolian desert land. The poet himself writes of his being "Originally a cotton-clothed of Lunhsi." That is to say, he was a plain citizen of a district in Kansu. But he was born, according to best authorities, in the adjoining land of Shuh, or the present Ssuchuan—that picturesque western province of mountains and tumbling waters which flow into the great Yangtze-kiang.

As to the year of his birth, biographers again differ. Some maintain it to have been as early as 699, while others would have it as late as 705, with consequent variation in his age, since he died, as all agree, in the year 762. A biographical calendar, compiled by Sieh Chung-yung of the Sung dynasty, places the poet's birth in the second year of the Shen-lung era; while another calendar by Wang-chi of the Ming dynasty, who edited the complete works of Li Po, fixes the year as the first of the Chang-an era. All evidence seems to favor the latter date, which falls in the year of 701.

On the night of the poet's birth his mother dreamed of the planet of Chang-keng, which is Venus, and which is popularly known in China as the *Tai-po Hsing*, meaning literally the *Great White Star*. Thus it was that he was named Po (the *White* One), and surnamed Tai-po (the *Great White* One). Later he dubbed himself the Green Lotus Man, borrowing the name from a Buddhist saint; and sometimes went by the self-evident designation of the "Old Wine Genius."

When a boy of six Li Po could read, and by the age of ten he had mastered the Confucian books of the *Odes* and the *History* and miscellaneous classics by a hundred writers, and was composing poems of his own. While he was still in his teens, he retired with a recluse by the name of Tunyen-tzu to the mountain of Min in northern Ssuchuan. Here the two men kept strange birds as pets and succeeded in taming them to feed from their hands, the report of which brought to their hermitage the local magistrate, who invited them to enter the government service. But they declined. Our young poet sang contentedly:

> For twenty springs I've lain among the clouds,
> Loving leisure and enamored of the hills.

In 721 he traveled down the Yangtze to Yun-meng, the land of seven moors, that lies to the north of the river and the Tung-ting Lake; here he was married to a granddaughter of a certain ex-minister Hsu, and stayed there for three years.

Then he moved up north to Shantung, and made his home in Jen-cheng and elsewhere. "I am thirty," he wrote to a friend, "I make verses without tiring, while in front of my house carts and horses go by." Years passed without any visible achievement. One cannot blame too harshly his first wife who, impatient of the lack of his promotion, left him with the children. It was during this period that he became one of the "Six Idlers of the Bamboo Valley" who gathered in the mountain of Chu-lai for the jolly fellowship of wine and song. He traveled extensively, too. Once he was in the city of Lo-yang, enjoying the lavish hospitality of Tung Tsas-chiu, who had a special wine house built for the poet at the Tien-tsin bridge-head, where

Songs were bought with yellow gold, and laughter with white jewels.[1]

Later the same host invited the poet to Ping-chou near Taiyuan-fu in Shansi, where Tung's father was stationed as the military commander. Here the two companions went on happy excursions, taking singing-girls out on the river by the dynastic shrine of Chin. It was in Ping-chou that the poet befriended Kuo Tsu-i, who was still a young soldier in the ranks, but who was later to become the savior of the empire as well as of the poet's life. In the year 738 Li Po was back in Shantung when Tu Fu, his one great and formidable rival in poetic fame, arrived in the province and met him. At once a warm friendship and exchange of poems began that lasted lifelong, and that makes the happiest and most memorable chapter in China's literary history. Tu Fu was the younger of the two. They slept together under one coverlet (so he tells us in one of his poems), and went hand in hand like two brothers.[2]

Li Po traveled south to the lands of Wu and Yueh of old to wander amid the ruins of once glorious palaces and among the lakes of lotus lilies, and chose to sojourn in a district called Yen, in Chehkiang, famous for the beauty of its hills and valleys. Here he met Wu Yun, scholar and Taoist, who on being summoned to court took Li Po with him to Chang-an, the capital of the empire.

It was about the year 742 that Li Po entered Chang-an, the golden metropolis, when the long prosperous years of the Tien-pao era had just begun, and the court of Hsuan Tsung had reached the pinnacle of brilliance. Li Po went to see Ho Chi-chang, a guest of the crown prince, and showed his poems. The jovial courtier was so pleased that he bartered his gold ornament for wine and entertained the new-comer. Moreover, he commended the poet to the emperor. "I have in my house," he said, "probably the greatest poet that ever existed. I have not dared to speak of him to your Majesty because of his one defect, which is rather difficult to correct: he drinks, and drinks sometimes to excess. But his poems are beautiful. Judge them for yourself, sire!" So saying, he thrust in Hsuan Tsung's hand a bundle of manuscript. "Fetch me the author of these poems!" spoke the emperor instantly—so runs one story.

But according to other versions it was Wu Yun, or Princess Yu-chen, who introduced Li Po to the court. At any rate, the poet was given an audience in the Hall of Gold Bells. His discourse and ode at once won the admiration of the emperor, so that he feasted the poet at the Table of the Seven Jewels and assigned him to the Han-ling Academy. That is, Li Po was placed under imperial patronage, without any special duties but to write occasional poems, of which the ninth piece in the present book is an example.

He banqueted with lords and ladies in and out of the court, and sought frequently the taverns of the city. But who were his boon companions? A vivid portrayal of that much

---

[1] See No. 59.
[2] See No. 127.

celebrated company, the "Eight Immortals of the Wine-cup," whose revels were the talk of Chang-an, is happily preserved for us in an equally celebrated poem by Tu Fu.

Chi-chang rides his horse, but reels
    As on a reeling ship.
Should he, blear-eyed, tumble into a well,
    He would lie in the bottom, fast asleep.
Ju-yang Prince must have three jugfuls
    Ere he goes up to court.
How copiously his royal mouth waters
    As a brewer's cart passes by!
It's a pity, he mournfully admits,
    That he is not the lord of Wine Spring.
Our minister *Li* squanders at the rate
    Of ten thousand *tsen* per day;
He inhales like a great whale,
    Gulping one hundred rivers;
And with a cup in his hand insists,
    He loves the *Sage* and avoids the Wise.
Tsung-chi a handsome youth, fastidious,
    Disdains the rabble,
But turns his gaze toward the blue heaven,
    Holding his beloved bowl.
Radiant is he like a tree of jade,
    That stands against the breeze.
Su Chin, the religious, cleanses his soul
    Before his painted Buddha.
But his long rites must needs be interrupted
    As oft he loves to go on a spree.
As for *Li Po*, give him a jugful,
    He will write one hundred poems.
He drowses in a wine-shop
    On a city street of Chang-an;
And though his sovereign calls,
    He will not board the imperial barge.
"Please your Majesty," says he,
    "I am a god of wine."
Chang Hsu is a calligrapher of renown,
    Three cups makes him the master.
He throws off his cap, baring his pate
    Unceremoniously before princes,
And wields his inspired brush, and lo!
    Wreaths of cloud roll on the paper.
Chao Sui, another immortal, elate
    After full five jugfuls,
Is eloquent of heroic speech—
    The wonder of all the feasting hall.

One day in spring Hsuan Tsung with Lady Yang Kuei-fei held a royal feast in the Pavilion of Aloes. The tree-peonies of the garden, newly imported from India, were in full flower as if in rivalry of beauty with the emperor's voluptuous mistress. There were the musicians of the Pear Garden and the wine of grapes from Hsi-liang. Li Po was summoned, for only his art could capture for eternity the glory of the vanishing hours. But when brought to the imperial presence, the poet was drunk. Court attendants threw cold water on his face and handed him a writing brush. Whereupon he improvised those three beautiful songs[3] in rapturous praise of Yang Kuei-fei, which were sung by the famous vocalist, Li Kuei-nien, while the emperor himself played the tune on a flute of jade.

But it was one of these very songs,[4] according to a widely accepted tradition, that helped cut short the gay and prodigal career of the poet at the court. Kao Li-shih, the powerful eunuch, who had been greatly humiliated by having been ordered to pull off Li Po's shoes once as the latter became drunk at the palace, persuaded Yang Kuei-fei that the poet had intended a malicious satire in his poem by comparing her with Lady Flying Swallow, who was a famous court beauty of the Han dynasty, but who was unfaithful and never attained the rank of empress. This was enough to turn gratitude to venomous hate, and Yang Kuei-fei interfered whenever the emperor sought to appoint the poet to office. There is another tradition that Li Po incurred the displeasure of Hsuan Tsung through the intrigue of a fellow courtier. This story is also plausible. Li Po was not the sort of man fitted for the highly artificial life of the court, where extreme urbanity, tact and dissimulation, were essential to success. He soon expressed a desire to return to the mountains; and the emperor presented him with a purse and allowed him to depart. He was then forty-five years old, and had sojourned in the capital for three years.

Once more Li Po took to the roads. He wandered about the country for ten years, "now sailing one thousand *li* in a day, now tarrying a whole year at a place, enjoying the beauty thereof." He went up northeast to Chinan-fu of Shantung to receive the Taoist diploma from the "high heavenly priest of Pei-hai." He journeyed south and met Tsui Tsung-chi, the handsome Immortal of the Wine-cup, who had been banished from the capitol and was an official at the city of Nanking. The old friendship was renewed, and withal the glad old time. It is related that one moonlight night they took a river journey down the Yangtze from Tsai-hsi to Nanking, during which Li Po arrayed himself in palace robes and sat in the boat, laughing aloud, and rolling his frenzied eyes. Was it the laughter of wanton revelry, or of self-derision, or of haughty scorn at the foolish world that could not fathom his soul? In 754 Wei Hao, a young friend of his, came to meet him at Kuang-ling, Kiangsu Province, and traveled with him a while. To him Li Po entrusted a bundle of his poems, saying, "Pray remember your old man! Surely in the future I'll acquire a great fame."

Next year, in March of 755, we discover him fleeing from the city of Lo-yang amid the confusion of the war of An Lu-shan, whose troops occupied the city and made the waters of the Lo River flow crimson with blood. The poet went down to the province of Chehkiang, and finally retired to the mountains of Luh near Kiu-kiang in Kiangsi Province. When Li Ling, the Prince of Yung, became the governor-general of the four provinces near the mouth of the Yangtze, Li Po joined his staff. But the subsequent revolt and the quick fall of the Prince in 757 lead to imprisonment of the poet at the city of Kiu-

---

[3] See No. 6, 7, & 8.
[4] See No. 7.

kiang, with a sentence of death hanging over him. On examination of the case officials were inclined to leniency. One of them, Sung Ssu-jo, recommended the emperor not only to pardon Li Po but to give him a high place in the government service. But the memorial, which by the way had been written by Li Po himself at Sung's direction, failed to reach its destination. Then Kuo Tsu-i, now a popular hero with his brilliant war record, came to the rescue; he petitioned that Li Po's life might be ransomed with his own rank and title. The white head of the poet was saved, and he was sentenced to perpetual banishment at Yeh-lang—the extreme southwest region of the empire covered by the present province of Yunnan.

He proceeded westward up the river leisurely. There seems to have been little pressure from the central government, certainly no inclination on the part of the poet, to expedite the journey. At Wu-chang he was welcomed by the local governor Wei, with whom he spent months and climbed the Yellow Crane House three times. Further up he encountered Chia-chi, his former companion at Chang-an, and Li Hua, a kinsman of his. These two had also been demoted and dismissed from the capital. The three luckless men now joined in a boat party more than once on the Tung-ting Lake under the clear autumn moon. That these were not so lugubrious affairs after all is attested by their poems.[5] After such delays and digressions Li Po sailed up the Yangtze through the Three Gorges and arrived in Wu-shan, Ssuchuan, in 759, when amnesty was declared.

> It was as if warmth enlivened the frozen vale,
> And fire and flame had sprung from dead ashes.[6]

The old poet started homeward, resting a while at Yo-chou and Chiang-hsia, and returning to Kiu-kiang again. He visited Nanking once more in 761; and next year went to live with his kinsman, Li Yang-ping, who was magistrate of Tang-tu, the present city of Taiping in Anhwei. Here in the same year he sickened and died.

A legend has it that Li Po was drowned in the river near Tsai-shih as he attempted, while drunken, to embrace the reflection of the moon in the water. This was further elaborated into a tale, which was translated by Théodore Pavie. This story, quoted by d'Hervey Saint Denys, is altogether too beautiful to omit. I retranslate the passage from the French:

"The moon that night was shining like day. Li Tai-po was supping on the river when all of a sudden there was heard in the mid-air a concert of harmonious voices, which sounded nearer and nearer to the boat. Then, the water rose in a great tumult, and lo! there appeared in front of Li Tai-po dolphins which stood on their tails, waving their fins, and two children of immortality carrying in their hands the banners to indicate the way. They had come in behalf of the lord of the heavens to invite the poet to return and resume his place in the celestial realm. His companions on the boat saw the poet depart, sitting on the back of a dolphin while the harmonious voices guided the cortege... Soon they vanished altogether in the mist."

As to Li Po's family and domestic life the curiosity of the western mind has to go unsatisfied. The Chinese biographers never bother about such trivialities of a man's

---

[5] See No. 52, 121, 122, & 128.
[6] See No. 124.

private affairs. The Old and the New Books of Tang are both totally silent. Only in his preface to the collection of the poet's works Wei Hao remarks:

"Po first married a Hsu and had a daughter and a son, who was called the Boy of the Bright Moon. The daughter died after her marriage. Po also took to wife a Liu. The Liu was divorced, and he next was united to a woman of Luh, by whom he had a child, named Po-li. He finally married a Sung."

Hsu, Liu, and Sung are all family names of the women who were successively married to Li Po. Of his several poems extant, addressed to his "wife," it is difficult to tell just which one is meant in each case. From a poem[7] written to his children we learn that the girl's name was Ping-yang, and the son whom Wei Hao refers to by the unusual nickname of the "Boy of the Bright Moon," was called Po-chin. Of the third child, Po-li, mentioned by Wei Hao, there is no reference elsewhere. Po-chin died without having obtained any official appointment in 793. His one son wandered away from home; while his two daughters were married to peasants.

Although Li Po had expressed his desire of making the Green Hill at a short distance southeast of Taiping-fu his last resting place, he was buried at the "East Base" of the Dragon Hill. His kinsman, Li Hua, wrote the inscription on his tombstone. Twenty-nine years after the poet's death a governor of Tang-tu set up a monument. But by the second decade of the ninth century when another great poet, Po Chu-i, came to visit the grave, he found it in the grass of a fallow field. About the same time Fan Chuan-cheng, inspector of these districts, discovered the "burial mound three feet high, fast crumbling away"; he located the two granddaughters of Li Po among the peasantry, and on learning the true wish of the poet, removed the grave to the north side of the Green Hill and erected two monuments in January of 818.

IV

The Old Book of Tang says that Li Po "possessed a superior talent, a great and tameless spirit, and fantastical ways of the transcendent mind." In modern terminology he was a romanticist.

Like Wordsworth he sought the solitude of hills and lakes. But he was a lover rather than a worshipper of Nature. He was "enamored of the hills," he says. To him the cloud-girt peak of Luh Shan, or the hollow glen of autumn, was not a temple but a home where he felt most at ease and free to do as he pleased—where he drank, sang, slept, and meditated. He spent a large part of his life out of doors, on the roads, among the flowering trees, and under the stars, writing his innumerable poems, which are the spontaneous utterances of his soul, responding, to the song of a mango bird or to the call of far waterfalls. And his intimate Nature-feeling gained him admission to a world other than ours, of which he writes:

Why do I live among the green mountains?
I laugh and answer not. My soul is serene.
It dwells in another heaven and earth belonging to no man—
The peach trees are in flower, and the water flows on...

---

[7] See No. 63.

Taoism with its early doctrine of inaction and with its later fanciful superstitions of celestial realms, and supernatural beings and of death-conquering herbs and pellets fascinated the poet. Confucian critics, eager to whitewash him of any serious Taoistic contamination, declare that he was simply playing with the new-fangled heresy. But there is no doubt as to his earnestness. "At fifteen," he writes, "I sought gods and goblins." The older he grew, the stronger became the hold of Taoism on his mind. In fact, the utilitarian principle of Confucian ethics was alien both to his temperament and to the circumstances of his life. The first thing he did after his dismissal from the court was to go to Chinan-fu and receive the Taoist diploma from the high priest of the sect, "wishing only (says Li Yang-ping) to return east to Peng-lai and with the winged men ride to the Scarlet Hill of Immortality." Peng-lai is the paradisical land of the Taoist, somewhere in the eastern sea. The poetry of Li Po reflects the gleams of such visionary worlds. His "Dream of the Sky-land,"[8] rivaling Kubla Khan in its transcendent beauty and imaginative power, could not have been written but by Li Po, the Taoist. Even in superstition and opium there is more than a Confucian philosophy dreams of.

But mysticism and solitude filled only one half of the poet's life. For he loved dearly the town and tavern— so much so that he is censured again by moralists as having been sordid. Li Po not only took too hearty an interest in wine and women, but he was also scandalously frank in advertising his delight by singing their praise in sweet and alluring terms. In this respect Li Po, like so many of his associates, was a thorough Elizabethan. Had the Eight Immortals of the Wine-cup descended from their Chinese Elysium to the Mermaid Tavern, how happy they would have been with their doughty rivals in song, humor, wit, capacity for wine, and ardent and adventurous, if at times erratic, spirit!

Li Po "ate like a hungry tiger," says Wei Hao, who should know; while according to another authority, "his big voice could be heard in heaven." In his early youth he exhibited a swashbuckling propensity, took to errantry, and learned swordmanship, and even slashed several combatants with his cutlass.

"Though less than seven feet in height, I am strong enough to meet ten thousand men," he boasted. It is hardly necessary, however, to point out the rare and lovable personality of the poet, who made friends with everybody—lord or prince, Buddhist or Taoist, courtier or scholar, country gentlemen or town brewer; and addressed with the same affectionate regard alike the emperor in the palace and the poor singing-girl on the city street of Chang-an.

In his mature age Li Po, despite his natural inclination and temperament, cherished the normal Chinese ambition to serve the state in a high official capacity and try the empire-builder's art.[9] It was with no small anticipation that he went to the court and discoursed on the affairs of the government before the emperor. But he was only allowed to write poems and cover his vexations with the cloak of dissipation. Later when amid the turmoil of the civil war he was called to join the powerful Prince of Yung, his aspirations revived, only to be smothered in the bitterness of defeat and banishment. The last few years of his life were pathetic. Broken in spirit and weary with the burden of sorrow and age, but with his patriotic fervor still burning in his heart, he watched with anxiety the sorry plight of his country.

---

[8] See No. 77.
[9] See No. 79. & 124.

In the middle of the night I sigh four or five times,
Worrying ever over the great empire's affairs.

The rebellion of An Lu-shan and its aftermath were not wholly quelled till the very year of the poet's death.

Then, there was the inevitable pessimism of the old world. The thought of the evanescence of all temporal things brought him solace for life's disappointments, and at the same time subdued his great tameless spirit. The Chinese race was already old at Li Po's time, with a retrospect of milleniums on whose broad expanse the dynasties of successive ages were like bubbles. What Shakespeare came to realize in his mellowed years about the "cloud-capt towers and gorgeous palaces," was an obsession that seized on Li Po early in life. Thus it is that a pensive mood pervades his poetry, and many of his Bacchanalian verses are tinged with melancholy. Even when he is singing exultantly at a banquet table, his saddest thought will out, saying "Hush, hush! All things pass with the waters of the east-flowing river."

POEMS BY LI PO

1. ON THE SHIP OF SPICE-WOOD

My ship is built of spice-wood and has a rudder of *mulan*;
Musicians sit at the two ends with jeweled bamboo flutes and pipes of gold.
What a pleasure it is, with a cask of sweet wine
And singing girls beside me,
To drift on the water hither and thither with the waves!
I am happier than the fairy of the air, who rode on his yellow crane.
And free as the merman who followed the sea-gulls aimlessly.
Now with the strokes of my inspired pen I shake the Five Mountains.
My poem is done, I laugh and my delight is vaster than the sea.
Oh, deathless poetry! The songs of Chu-ping are ever glorious as the sun and
	moon,
While the palaces and towers of the Chu kings have vanished from the hills.
Yea, if worldly fame and riches were things to last forever,
The waters of the River Han would flow north-westward, too.

The poet is in his typical mood. The poem is a manifesto of his happy triumphant existence of freedom and of sensual and poetical indulgence.

Mu-lan is the name of a precious wood.

Chu-ping, or Chu Yuan, 332-295 B. C., was a loyal minister under Huai-wang, the ruler of the Chu state. He is celebrated for his poems, which include the famous Li Sao.

The river Han is a large tributary of the Yangtze, which originates in Shensi and flows southwestward through Hupeh, joining the main stream at Hankow.

2. A SUMMER DAY

Naked I lie in the green forest of summer....
Too lazy to wave my white feathered fan.
I hang my cap on a crag,
And bare my head to the wind that comes
Blowing through the pine trees.

3. NOCTURNE

Blue water... a clear moon...
In the moonlight the white herons are flying.
Listen! Do you hear the girls who gather water-chestnuts?
They are going home in the night, singing.

4. A FAREWELL SONG OF WHITE CLOUDS

The white clouds float over the mountains of Chu—
As over the mountains of Chin.
Everywhere the white clouds will follow you on.

They will follow you on everywhere—
With you they will enter the Chu mountains,
And cross the waters of the Hsiang.

Yonder across the waters of the Hsiang,
There is a cloak of ivy to wear,
And you may lie in a bed of white clouds.

Go swiftly home, O my friend!

5. THE LONG-DEPARTED LOVER

Fair one, when you were here, I filled the house with flowers.
Fair one, now you are gone—only an empty couch is left.
On the couch the embroidered quilt is rolled up; I cannot sleep.
It is three years since you went. The perfume you left behind haunts me still.

The perfume strays about me forever, but where are you, Beloved?
I sigh—the yellow leaves fall from the branch,
I weep—the dew twinkles white on the green mosses.

6. LADY YANG KUEI-FEI AT THE IMPERIAL FEAST OF THE PEONY—I

The glory of trailing clouds is in her garments,
And the radiance of a flower on her face.
O heavenly apparition, found only far above
On the top of the Mountain of Many Jewels,
Or in the fairy Palace of Crystal when the moon is up!
Yet I see her here in the earth's garden—
The spring wind softly sweeps the balustrade,
And the dew-drops glisten thickly....

As to the occasion on which these songs were composed, see the Introduction.
The Mountain of Many Jewels is the abode of the fairy queen, Hsi-wang-mo; the Palace of Crystal is another such fabled home of beautiful spirits.

7. LADY YANG KUEI-FEI AT THE IMPERIAL FEAST OF THE PEONY—II

She is the flowering branch of the peony,
Richly-laden with honey-dew.
Hers is the charm of the vanished fairy,
That broke the heart of the dreamer king
In the old legend of the Cloud and Rain.
Pray, who in the palace of Han
Could be likened unto her,
Save the lady, Flying Swallow, newly-dressed
In all her loveliness?

The Legend of Cloud and Rain: King Hsiang of Chu once in his dream saw a fairy maid whose loveliness captivated his heart instantly, and who, on being asked who she was, replied, "In the morning I am the cloud, in the evening the rain on the Wu mountains," and vanished. The amorous king pined for the cloud and rain, morning and evening ever after.

Chao Fei-yen or Lady Flying Swallow, was a singing girl of Chang-an, but her charm won the love of the emperor Cheng-ti of the Han dynasty, who took her up to the palace and made her an imperial concubine of the highest rank. She is famous for her frail beauty. It is said that she was of so slight a build that she could dance on the palm of the hand. She lived in the 1st century B. C.

8. LADY YANG KUEI-FEI AT THE IMPERIAL FEAST OF THE PEONY—III

She stands, leaning against the balustrade
Of Chen-hsiang Ting, the Pavilion of Aloes.
Vanquished are the endless longings of Love
Borne into the heart on the wind of spring.
The radiant flower and the flowery queen rejoice together,
For the emperor deigns to watch them ever with a smile.

9. A POEM COMPOSED AT THE IMPERIAL COMMAND IN THE SPRING GARDEN, WHILE LOOKING ON THE NEWLY GREEN WILLOWS BY THE DRAGON POND AND LISTENING TO THE HUNDRED-FOLD NOTES OF THE FIRST NIGHTINGALES

The east wind blowing, the grass of Ying-chow is green;
The spring-sweetness is about the purple palaces and crimson towers.
The willows on the south of the pond have turned half-green,
They grow like delicate wreaths of mist
By the resplendent castle,
Their thread-like branches, one hundred feet long,
Dangling about the carved and painted pillars.
While high above the sweet birds sing melodiously together—
They sing with hearts stirred early by the spring wind,
Which rolls itself in the blue clouds and dies.

The voice of spring is heard all over—
By a thousand gateways and by ten thousand doorways.
At Hao-king, where my lord, the emperor, tarries,
Five colored clouds are brightening
Against the lucid purple of the sky.
The imperial cortege comes forth, agleam in the sun.
Coming forth from the golden palace,
The imperial car bedecked with jewels
Glides along the path of flowers,
First turning to the Peng-lai Garden,
Where cranes are seen gracefully dancing,
Then, returning to the garden of Yi-shih,
Where the first songs of nightingales are heard—
They sing high among the trees,
Desiring to mingle their notes with the mouth-organs,
And join the imperial concert of the phoenix-flutes.

Hao-king is an old name for Chang-an, the capital.

10. TO HIS FRIEND DEPARTING FOR SHUH

I hear the Tsang-tsung road
Is rough and rugged, and hard to travel.
It is so steep that the mountains rise
In front of the rider's face,
And the clouds gather about the horse's head.
But there you will find the plank-highway of Chin
Canopied in fragrant foliage,
And the sweet water of springtime
Flowing around the city wall of Shuh.
Go, my friend! Our destiny's decided…
You need not bother to ask Chuan-ping, the fortune-teller.

Tsan-tsung is one of the mythical rulers of Shuh, or the present Ssuchuan.

Chuan-ping teas a fortune teller of Chengtu under the Han dynasty. As soon as he had earned a hundred pence, he would close his shop and busy himself with writing books.

11. TO HIS THREE FRIENDS

When the hunter sets traps only for rabbits,
Tigers and dragons are left uncaught.
Even so, men of blue-cloud ambition remain unsought,
Singing aloud at the door of their rocky den.

My friend, Han, you are rare and profound;
Pei, you possess a true clean breast;
And Kung, you, too, are an excellent man;
And all you three are lovers of cloud and mist.
Your stout and straight souls
Are loftier than the loftiest pine.
A flat boulder for a bed, you sleep together under one cover;
You hack the ice and sip water from the winter stream;
You own two pairs of shoes to wear among you three.

Once wandering as you please
Like the vagrant clouds,
You came out of the mountains to greet the governor.
Indifferently you wore cap and mantle a while,
Whistling long.

Last night you dreamed of returning to your old haunt,
And enjoying, you say, the moon of the Bamboo Valley.
This morning outside the east gate of Luh
We spread the tent and drink the farewell cup.

Be careful as you go!
The cliffs are snowy, and your horses may slip;

And the road of tangled vines may perplex you.
Pray remember,
My thoughts of longing are like the smoke grass,
That grows always in profusion, winter or spring!

The three friends were Han Chun, Pei Cheng, and Kung Chao-fu, all of whom were members of the "Six Idlers of the Bamboo Valley." These men were returning to the mountains after a brief and unsuccessful official career under the local governor, and Li Po wrote this parting poem.

12. ADDRESSED HUMOROUSLY TO TU FU

Here! is this you on the top of Fan-ko Mountain,
Wearing a huge hat in the noon-day sun?
How thin, how wretchedly thin, you have grown!
You must have been suffering from poetry again.

In contrast with Li Po, who depended largely on inspiration, Tu Fu was a painstaking artist careful of the minutest details.

13. ON A PICTURE SCREEN

Whence these twelve peaks of Wu-shan!
Have they flown into the gorgeous screen
From heaven's one corner?

Ah, those lonely pines murmuring in the wind!
Those palaces of Yang-tai, hovering yonder—
Oh, the melancholy of it!—
Where the jeweled couch of the king
With brocade covers is desolate,—
His elfin maid voluptuously fair
Still haunting them in vain!

Here a few feet
Seem a thousand miles,
The craggy walls glisten blue and red,
A piece of dazzling embroidery.
How green those distant trees are
Round the river strait of Ching-men!
And those ships—they go on,
Floating on the waters of Pa.
The water sings over the rocks
Between countless hills
Of shining mist and lustrous grass.

How many years since these valley flowers bloomed
To smile in the sun?
And that man traveling on the river,
Hears he not for ages the monkeys screaming?
Whoever looks on this,
Loses himself in eternity;
And entering the sacred mountains of Sung,
He will dream among the resplendent clouds.

The screen was owned by his Buddhist friend, Yuan Tan-chiu, to whom Li Po has written innumerable poems. See No. 99.

The Wu-shan peaks are along the Yangtze gorges in Ssuchuan. The second stanza refers to the Legend of the Cloud and Rain. See the note under No. 7.

14. ON ASCENDING THE NORTH TOWER ONE AUTUMN DAY

The waterside city stands as in a picture scroll.
The sky is lucid above the mountain shrouded in evening gloom,
While the waters on either hand shine like mirrors;
Two painted bridges span them like rainbows dropt from the sky.
The smoke from the cottages curls up around the citron trees,
And the hues of late autumn are on the green paulownias.
Who ever dreamed of my coming hither to the North Tower
To brood over the memory of Prince Hsieh, while the wind blows in my face?

The North Tower was built by Hsieh Tiao of the 5th century, a statesman and a poet of South Chi dynasty. It is located in the city of Hsuan-cheng, Anhwei.

15. THE SUMMIT TEMPLE

To-night I stay at the Summit Temple.
Here I could pluck the stars with my hand,
I dare not speak aloud in the silence,
For fear of disturbing the dwellers of heaven.

The temple is in a district in Hupeh, so isolated from the outside world that this poem of Li Po, written on a painted board and left on the beams of the ceiling, remained unmolested for centuries until it was discovered by a local magistrate, thus settling a dispute over its authorship which had arisen in the meantime, some attributing the poem to a certain Yang, who was born mute—the story runs—but on being taken to a high tower one day when he was only a boy of a few years, composed and uttered this poem, of which the first line reads:
"A precipitous tower, one hundred feet high!"

16. LAO-LAO TING, A TAVERN

Here friends come, sorrowing, to say farewell,
O Lao-lao Ting, tavern where every heart must ache.
Here even the wind of spring knows the pain of parting,
And will not let the willow branches grow green.

The tavern was situated on a hill-top just outside the city of Nanking; and people seeing their friends off came as far as this place to exchange parting cups.
The last line alludes to the Chinese custom of breaking off a willow branch and presenting it to a departing friend.

17. THE NIGHT OF SORROW

A lovely woman rolls up
The delicate bamboo blind.
She sits deep within,
Twitching her moth eyebrows.
Who may it be
That grieves her heart?
On her face one sees
Only the wet traces of tears.

18. THE SORROW OF THE JEWEL STAIRCASE

The dew is white upon the staircase of jewels,
And wets her silken shoes. The night is far gone.
She turns within, lets fall the crystal curtain,
And gazes up at the autumn moon, shining through.

19. THE GIRL OF PA SPEAKS

The water of the River Pa is swift like an arrow;
The boat on the River Pa slips away
As if it had wings.
It will travel in ten days three thousand *li*.
And you are going, my dear—
Ah, how many years before you return?

Pa is the eastern region of Ssuchuan, traversed by the swift flowing Yangtze.

20. THE WOMEN OF YUEH—I

She is a southern girl of Chang-kan Town;
Her face is prettier than star or moon,
And white like frost her feet in sandals—
She does not wear the crow-head covers.

In these poems Li Po records what he saw of the "southern" girls in Kiangsu and Chehkiang. These provinces were under the king of Yueh in the 5th and 6th centuries, B. C.

Chang-kan is near the city of Nanking, and was at Li Po's time inhabited by the lower class of people.

The crowhead covers are a kind of shoes worn by the upper-class women of the north. So named on account of their shape and very small size—small feet seem to have been already at a premium. "It is interesting," remarks a native critic demurely, "to note Li Po's admiration for a barefoot woman."

21. THE WOMEN OF YUEH—II

Many a girl of the south is white and lucent.
Often she will steer her shallop and play.
In her coquettish eyes
Lurks the lure of the spring-time.
She will pluck the flowers of the water
For amorous wayfarers.

22. THE WOMEN OF YUEH—III

She is gathering lotus in the river of Yeh.
She spies a passer-by, and turns round,
Singing her boat song.
She laughs, and hides away among the lilies;
And seeming shy, she will not show her face again.

23. THE WOMEN OF YUEH—IV

She, a Tung-yang girl, stands barefoot on the bank
He, a boatman of Kuei-chi, is in his boat.
The moon has not set. They look at each other—broken-hearted.

24. THE WOMEN OF YUEH—V

The water of the Mirror Lake
Is clear like the moon.
The girl of Yeh-chi
Has a face white as snow.
Her silvery image
Trembles in the silvery ripple…

25. THE SOLITUDE OF NIGHT

It was at a wine party—
I lay in a drowse, knowing it not.
The blown flowers fell and filled my lap.
When I arose, still drunken,
The birds had all gone to their nests,
And there remained but few of my comrades.
I went along the river—alone in the moonlight.

26. THE MONUMENT OF TEARS

The mountain of Hsien looks down on the Han River;
The water is blue and its sand shines like snow.
There on the mountain top stands the Monument of Tears,
Long weathered and covered up with green mosses.

The Mountain of Hsien is in Hupeh, near the city of Hsiang-yang. Once in the reign of the Chin dynasty (3rd century), Yang Hu, the governor of this district, a man of benevolence, climbed the mountain to view the fair landscape below. Amid the feasting and verse-making, the governor turned to his companions and said: "This mountain has stood here since the beginning of the world; and many famous men of virtue and wisdom have come up to this spot, as we ourselves. Now they are all gone and forgotten. Soon we shall be, too." So saying, he shed tears. Later the people erected a monument there. It is this that Li Po found "covered up with green mosses."

27. ON A QUIET NIGHT

I saw the moonlight before my couch,
And wondered if it were not the frost on the ground.
I raised my head and looked out on the mountain moon;
I bowed my head and thought of my far-off home.

28. THE BLUE WATER

Blue is the water and clear the moon,
He is out on the South Lake,
Gathering white lilies,
The lotus flowers seem to whisper love,
And fill the boatman's heart with sadness.

29. THE CHING-TING MOUNTAIN

Flocks of birds have flown high and away;
A solitary drift of cloud, too, has gone, wandering on.
And I sit alone with the Ching-ting Peak, towering beyond.
We never grow tired of each other, the mountain and I.

The Ching-ting mountain is situated to the north of the city of Hsuan-cheng, Anhwei.

30. WITH A MAN OF LEISURE

Yonder the mountain flowers are out.
We drink together, you and I.
One more cup—one more cup—still one more cup!
Now I am drunk and drowsy, you had better go.
But come to-morrow morning, if you will, with the harp!

31. THE YO-MEI MOUNTAIN MOON

The autumn moon is half round above the Yo-mei Mountain;
Its pale light falls in and flows with the water of the Ping-chiang River.
To-night I leave Ching-chi of the limpid stream for the Three Canyons,
And glide down past Yu-chow, thinking of you whom I can not see.

This is one of the most famous poems in all Chinese literature; and it is needless to say that the translation does a gross injustice to the original verse, which combines the beauty of a fluent language with the wealth of charming associations that the proper names possess, which, by the way, take up 12 of the 28 ideographs that compose the whole poem.
The mountain and stream are all located in Ssuchuan.

32. ON THE CITY STREET

They meet in the pink dust of the city street.
He raises his gold crop high in salute.
"Lady," says he, "where do you live?
"There are ten thousand houses among the drooping willow trees."

33. ON THE DEATH OF THE GOOD BREWER OF HSUAN-CHENG

So, old man, you're down where the yellow waters flow.
Well, I imagine you are still brewing the "Old Spring-time"
But since there's no Li Po on the Terrace of Night,
To what sort of people do you sell your wine?

A Chinese tradition has it that in Hades there is a spring, whose water is yellow. "The Yellow Spring" in Chinese has long become a proper name, referring to the world beyond.
"Terrace of Night" is another Chinese phrase for the land of the dead.
"The Old Springtime," a brand of rice wine. The Tang people named their rice wine frequently after the season of spring. Tu Fu mentions a "Rice Spring."

34. TO HIS WIFE

Three hundred sixty days a year
Drunk I lie, like mud every day.
Though you're married to Tai-po, wife,
You might as well have been the Tai-chang's spouse.

Tai-chang is the title of a religious officer in the government of the Han dynasty. Here a Tai-chang of the latter Han dynasty is alluded to, who was noted for his wine-bibbing propensity.

35. THE POET THINKS OF HIS OLD HOME

I have not turned my steps toward the East Mountain for so long.
I wonder how many times the roses have bloomed there...
The white clouds gather and scatter again like friends.
Who has a house there now to view the setting of the bright moon?

*The East Mountain (Tung Shan), in Chehkiang. Hsieh An, the poet-governor of the
4th century under the Chin dynasty, whom Li Po admired immensely, had resided here.*

36. SORROW OF THE LONG GATE PALACE—I

The Northern Dipper has turned round in the sky,
And now hangs over the west tower.
In the Golden House there are none
Save the fireflies sailing the gloom,
While the moonlight falls
Into the Palace of Long Gate,
And deepens still more the sorrow of one in the secret bower.

*Lady Chen who was queen to Wu-ti, a Han emperor, lost his favor and was left in the
solitude of the Long Palace Gate to pine alone. Later at the imperial harem of China, the
"Sorrow of the Long Gate" became a stock-phrase and served as a title for love poems of
grief under similar circumstances.*
The Northern Dipper, i. e. Ursa Major.
The Golden House always refers to a palace for the fair sex.

37. SORROW OF THE LONG GATE PALACE—II

The glad spring goes unattended
At the laurel bower where sorrow is long;
But on the four walls of gold
The autumn dust clings like grief;
And night holds the bright mirror up in the emerald sky
For the lonely one in the Palace of Long Gate.

38. AN ENCOUNTER IN THE FIELD

Came an amorous rider,
Trampling the fallen flowers of the road.
The dangling end of his crop
Brushes a passing carriage of five-colored clouds.
The jeweled curtain is raised,
A beautiful woman smiles within—
"That is my house," she whispers,
Pointing to a pink house beyond.

39. TO WANG LUN

I was about to sail away in a junk,
When suddenly I heard
The sound of stamping and singing on the bank—
It was you and your friends come to bid me farewell.
The Peach Flower Lake is a thousand fathoms deep,
But it cannot compare, O Wang Lun
With the depth of your love for me.

The Peach Flower Lake is the name of the water as well as of the village on its shore. Here Li Po spent some time, enjoying the hospitality of Wang Lun who had always a supply of good wine. At the departure of the poet the host came out to the waterside to bid farewell in the manner described in the poem.

40. ON SEEING OFF MENG HAO-JAN

My friend bade farewell at the Yellow Crane House,
And went down eastward to Willow Valley
Amid the flowers and mists of March.
The lonely sail in the distance
Vanished at last beyond the blue sky.
And I could see only the river
Flowing along the border of heaven.

The Yellow Crane House stood till a recent date not far from the city of Wu-chang, Hupeh, on a hill overlooking the Yangtze-kiang.

Once upon a time a dead man of Shuh, traveling on the back of a yellow crane, stopped here to rest. Hence the name of the house.

There is another interesting story just as authentic, according to which: there stood here a tavern kept by a man whose name was Chin, to whom one day a tall rugged professor in rags came and asked very complacently, "I haven't money, will you give me wine?" The tavern keeper was game; he readily offered to the stranger the biggest tumbler and allowed him to help himself to all the wine he wanted day after day for half a year. At last the professor said to Chin, "I owe you some wine money. I'll pay you now." So saying, he took lemon peels and with it smeared on the wall a picture of a yellow crane, which at the clapping of his hands came to life and danced to the tune of his song. The spectacle soon brought a fortune to the tavern-keeper; he became a millionaire. Then, the professor left, flying away on his bird, whither no one knew. The grateful tavern-keeper built the tower-house in commemoration thereof, and called it the Yellow Crane House.

Willow Valley (Yang-chow), in Kiangsu.

41. ON BEING ASKED WHO HE IS

I call myself the Green Lotus Man;
I am a spirit exiled from the upper blue;
For thirty years I've hid my fame in wine shops.
Warrior of Lake Province, why must you ask about me?
Behold me, a reincarnation of the Buddha of Golden Grain!

*The Warrior of Lake Province happened to be a Buddhist and the speaker of the
assembly of his sect. Hence, Li Po's witticism in referring to the Buddhist theology.*

42. IN THE MOUNTAINS

Why do I live among the green mountains?
I laugh and answer not, my soul is serene:
It dwells in another heaven and earth belonging to no man.
The peach trees are in flower, and the water flows on...

43. THE FAIR QUEEN OF WU

The breeze passes through the lotus flowers—
All fragrance is the waterside pavilion.
The king of Wu is feasting on the Ku-su Tower.
Hsi-shih, the queen, flushed with wine, dances—
She is fair and unresisting.
Now, smiling, she leans near the east window
Against a couch of white jade.

*Hsi-shih (5th century B. C.) was queen to Fu Chai, the king of Wu, and is one of the
most famous court beauties of China. Her dalliance cost the king his kingdom as well as
his life.*

44. WHILE JOURNEYING

The delicious wine of Lan-ling is of golden hue and flavorous.
Come, fill my precious glass, and let it glow in amber!
If you can only make me drunk, mine host, it is enough;
No longer shall I know the sorrow of a strange land.

Lan-ling, in Shantung.

45. THE RUIN OF THE KU-SU PALACE

In the deserted garden among the crumbling walls
The willows show green again,
While the sweet notes of the water-nut song
Seem to lament the spring.
Nothing remains but the moon above the river—
The moon that once shone on the fair faces
That smiled in the king's palace of Wu.

The Ku-su Palace is where King Fu-chai of Wu with his beautiful queen Hsi-shih held perpetual revelries till King Kou Chien of Yueh annihilated him. It was located in the present city of Soo Chow, which was the capital of Wu. See No. 43.

46. THE RUIN OF THE CAPITAL OF YUEH

Hither returned Kou Chien, the King of Yueh, in triumph;
He had destroyed the kingdom of Wu.
His loyal men came home in brilliance of brocade,
And the women of the court thronged the palace
Like flowers that fill the spring—
Now only a flock of partridges are flying in the twilight.

See Nos. 44 and 45.

47. THE RIVER JOURNEY FROM WHITE KING CITY

At dawn I left the walled city of White King,
Towering among the many colored clouds;
And came down stream in a day
One thousand *li* to Chiang-ling.
The screams of monkeys on either bank
Had scarcely ceased echoing in my ear
When my skiff had left behind it
Ten thousand ranges of hills.

The White King City is in Ssuchuan, and Chiang-ling in Hupeh. The distance between the two places is several hundred miles, but the river flows so swiftly that the down stream journey may be accomplished in a day.

48. BY THE GREAT WALL—I

Came the barbarian horde with the autumn;
Out went the imperial army from the House of Han.
The general has divided the tiger tallies,
And the dunes of White Dragon are now
The camping ground of the brave.
The moon in the wilderness
Follows the movement of his bow,
And upon his sword the desert frost blossoms.
He has not even entered this side of the Jewel Gate Pass.
But do not heave a long sigh, O little wife!

These poems tell the longing and the sorrow of young wives, whose husbands are fighting the barbarians in a distant land—a common theme for Tang poets.

The tiger tallies were used as a means of army registration. These were distributed among the soldiers prior to their departure for the front, while the counterparts were preserved at the headquarters.

The Jewel Gate Pass in western Kansu was located, according to the old Chinese geography, 3600 li *west of Chang-an.*

49. BY THE GREAT WALL—II

He rides his white charger by the Fortalice of Gold,
She wanders in dreams amid the desert cloud and sand.
It is a season of sorrow that she scarce can endure,
Thinking of her soldier lover at the border fort.
The fireflies, flitting about, swarm at her window,
While the moon slowly passes over her solitary bower.
The leaves of the green paulonia are tattered;
And the branches of the sha-tung blasted and sere.
There is not an hour but she, alone, unseen,
Weeps—only to learn how futile all her tears are.

50. THE IMPERIAL CONCUBINE

When a little child,
She was reared in a golden house,
Now ripe and lovely, she dwells
In the imperial palace of purple.
She will come forth from the innermost chamber,
A mountain flower in her glossy hair,
Robed in pink embroidered silk;
And always return at evening,
Accompanying the imperial palanquin.
Only, alas!— the hours of dance and song
Swiftly vanish into the sky
To tint, perhaps, the flying clouds in happy colors!

One of the eight poems entitled "Palace Pleasures," which Li Po composed during his sojourn at the court. They describe the voluptuous life of Hsuan Tsung with Yang Kuei-fei.

51. PARTING AT CHING-MEN

Faring far across the river-narrow of Ching-men
I have come with you into the land of Chu.
Here ends the mountain-range that stretches along the plain,
While the river flowing on, enters the distant heavens.
Now under the moon like a mirror flying through the sky,
And the rising clouds that build palaces and towers,
I bid you farewell. Ten thousand *li* you sail away,
But it is the waters of the home river that bear you on.

52. ON THE YO-YANG TOWER WITH HIS FRIEND, CHIA

Here from this tower we may view
The whole fair region of Yo-yang,
And the winding river
Opening into the Tung-ting Lake.

O wild geese, flying past,
Take away with you the sorrow of the heart!
And, come, thou mountain, give us thy happy moon!

Here will we sit to feast
And tarry a while with the clouds
And pass the cup high above the world of cares.

When we are goodly warm with wine,
Then, thou cooling breeze, arise!
Come and blow as we dance!
And our sleeves will flap like wings.

The Yo-yang Tower is situated in Yo-chou, Hunan province.
The poem was probably written while on his way to Yeh-lang, the place of his
banishment. (See Nos. 121 and 122)

53. AWAKENING FROM SLEEP ON A SPRING DAY

Life is an immense dream. Why toil?
All day long I drowse with wine,
And lie by the post at the front door.
Awakening, I gaze upon the garden trees,
And, hark, a bird is singing among the flowers.
Pray, what season may this be?
Ah, the songster's a mango-bird,
Singing to the passing wind of spring.
I muse and muse myself to sadness,
Once more I pour my wine, and singing aloud,
Await the bright moonrise.
My song is ended—
What troubled my soul?—I remember not.

54. THREE WITH THE MOON AND HIS SHADOW

With a jar of wine I sit by the flowering trees.
I drink alone, and where are my friends?
Ah, the moon above looks down on me;
I call and lift my cup to his brightness.
And see, there goes my shadow before me.
Hoo! We're a party of three, I say,—
Though the poor moon can't drink,
And my shadow but dances around me,
We're all friends to-night,
The drinker, the moon and the shadow.
Let our revelry be meet for the spring time!

I sing, the wild moon wanders the sky.
I dance, my shadow goes tumbling about.
While we're awake, let us join in carousal;
Only sweet drunkenness shall ever part us.
Let us pledge a friendship no mortals know,
And often hail each other at evening
Far across the vast and vaporous space!

55. AN EXHORTATION

Do you not see the waters of the Yellow River
Come flowing from the sky?
The swift stream pours into the sea and returns nevermore.
Do you not see high on yonder tower
A white-haired one sorrowing before his bright mirror?
In the morning those locks were like black silk,
In the evening they are all snow.
Let us, while we may, taste the old delights,
And leave not the gold cask of wine
To stand alone in the moonlight!

Gods have bestowed our genius on us;
They will also find its use some day.
Be not loath, therefore, to spend
Even a thousand gold pieces!
Your money will come back.
Kill the sheep, slay the ox, and carouse!
Truly you should drink three hundred cups in a round!

Come, Chin, my friend!
Dear Tan-chiu, too.
To you I offer wine, you must not refuse it.
Now I will sing a snatch of song. Lend ear and hearken!
Little I prize gongs and drums and sweet-meats,
I desire only the long ecstasy of wine,
And desire not to awaken.

Since the days of old, the wise and the good
Have been left alone in their solitude,
While merry drinkers have achieved enviable fame.
The king of Chen would feast in ancient days
At his Palace of Peace and Pleasure;
Ten thousand measures of wine there were,
And reckless revelry forever.

Now let you and me buy wine to-day!
Why say we have not the price?
My horse spotted with five flowers,
My fur-coat worth a thousand pieces of gold,
These I will take out, and call my boy
To barter them for sweet wine.
And with you twain, let me forget
The sorrow of ten thousand ages!

56. THE INTRUDER

The grass of Yen is growing green and long
While in Chin the leafy mulberry branches hang low.
Even now while my longing heart is breaking,
Are you thinking, my dear, of coming back to me?

—O wind of spring, you are a stranger,
Why do you enter through the silken curtains of my bower?

57. THE CROWS AT NIGHTFALL

In the twilight of yellow clouds
The crows seek their nests by the city wall.
The crows are flying home, cawing—
Cawing to one another in the tree-tops.
Lo, the maid of Chin-chuan at her loom
Weaving brocade,—for whom, I wonder?
She murmurs softly to herself
Behind the blue mist of gauze curtain.
She stops her shuttle, and broods sadly,
Remembering him who is far away—
She must lie alone in her bower at night,
And her tears fall like rain.

The theme of this poem is a well-known story of a young wife, who was left alone in Chang-an by her husband while he lived in another city with his mistress. The deserted wife composed poems of her love and fidelity, and weaving them into a piece of brocade, sent it to her husband, who was so moved thereby that he called her to his side and lived with her in happiness ever after.
Chin Chuan is an old name of Chang-an.

58. TO MENG HAO-JAN

I like you, my friend, Meng,
Your love of beauty is something known
To everybody under heaven.
When young with red cheeks,
You cast aside your carriage and cap;
Now that your head is white,
You lie among the pine trees and the clouds.
You get drunk with the moon
As often as with the transparent wine;
And to the honor of serving the emperor
You prefer the rapture of blossoms.
Your nobility looms up like a high mountain,
Too high for others to attain to;

But they may breathe the rare fragrance
That your soul imparts.

Meng Hao-jan was a native of Hupeh and a poet of no mean reputation, ranking next to Li Po and Tu Fu in the entire galaxy of the poets of the glorious Tang period. He died in 740.

59. TO TUNG TSAO-CHIU

Tung Tsao-chiu of Lo-yang, friend,
I remember the good old time.
You built me a wine house to the south of the Tien-chin Bridge
Songs were bought with yellow gold, and laughter with white jewels.
Months went by in one long lasting rapture; we scorned kings and princes.

Wise and valiant men from all shores were there as your guests.
Among them I was your special friend, you had my heart's devotion.
For you I would not have declined to uproot mountains and overturn the sea.
To you I bared my heart and soul without hesitation.

I journeyed to Hwai-nan to dwell in the laurel grove;
You remained in the north of Lo, with many sad dreams.
The separation was more than we could bear,
So we met again and went together.

We went together a long way to Hsien-cheng
Through the thirty-six turns of the river, winding round and round,
And amid the voices of the pine wind over the innumerable cliffs,
Which having ceased—lo!
We burst into a valley—into the light of a thousand flowers.

There on the level ground with their horses of golden reins and silver saddles
Stood the governor of Han-tung and his men, who had come to meet us.
The Taoist initiates of Tzu-yang welcomed us, too, blowing on their jeweled
    bamboo pipes.
They took us on the Tower of Mist-Feasting,—what a music there stirred!
Such celestial notes! It seemed all the sacred birds of heaven sang together.
With those pipes playing, our long sleeves began to flap lightly.
At last the governor of Han-chung, drunken, rose and danced.
It was he, who covered me with his brocade robe;
And I, drunk too, chose his lap for pillow and went to sleep.
During the feast our spirits soared high over the ninth heaven,
But ere the morning we were scattered like stars and rain,
Scattered hither and thither, the Pass of Chu separating us wide,
As I sought my old nest in the mountains,
And you returned to your home across the Bridge of Wei.

Your honorable father brave as leopard and tiger
Became the governor of Ping-chow then.
And stopt the barbarian invasion.
In May you called me and I crossed the mountain of Tai-hsing.
My cart wheels were broken on the steep passes, winding like sheep guts; but
that did not matter.

I traveled on and came to Pe-liang and stayed for months.
What hospitality! What squandering of money!
Red jade cups and rare dainty food on tables inlaid with green jems!
You made me so rapturously drunk that I had no thought of returning.

Oft we went out to the western edge of the city,
To the Temple of Chin, where the stream was clear as emerald;
Where on a skiff afloat we played with water and made music on pipes and
drums;
Where the tiny waves looked like dragon-scales—and how green were the reed
in the shallows!
Pleasure-inspired, we took singing girls and gaily sailed the stream up and
down.
How beautiful are their vermilioned faces, when half-drunken, they turn to the
setting sun,
While the willow flakes are flying about them like snow,
And their green eyebrows are mirrored in the clear water one hundred feet deep!

And comelier still are the green eyebrows when the new moon shines.
The beautiful girls sing anew and dance in robes of thin silk.
Their songs, lifted by the zephyr, pass away in the sky,
But the sweet notes seem to linger in the air, hovering about the wandering
clouds.

The delight of those days cannot be had again.
I went west and offered my *Ode of the Long Willows*,
But to my skyey ambition the imperial gates were closed.
I came back to the East Mountain, white-headed.

I met you once more at the south end of the Bridge of Wei;
But once more we parted company north of Tsan-tai.
You ask me the measure of my sorrow—
Pray, watch the fast falling flowers at the going of spring!
I would speak, but speech could not utter all,
Nor is there an end to my heart's grief.
I call my boy and bid him kneel down and seal this letter,
And I send it to you a thousand miles, remembering.

This poem was written shortly after Li Po's departure from the capital, and tells of the companionship and excursions the poet had enjoyed with Tung Tsao-chiu before his going to the court. He is now a disappointed man, wandering over the country. See the Introduction.

Tung Tsao-chiu was a military official at Chiao district in northern Anhwei not very far from the city of Loyang.

Ping-chou, in central Shansi. The dynastic temple of Chin is located near the city of Taiyuan-fu. This locality was also called Pe-Liang.

The Ode of the Long Willows *was composed by the celebrated scholar and philosopher, Yang-Hsiung (B. C. 53—A. D. 18) of the Han dynasty. Here Li Po refers metaphorically to his own verse. The passage tells of his failure at the court.*

60. TAKING LEAVE OF A FRIEND

Blue mountains lie beyond the north wall;
Round the city's eastern side flows the white water.
Here we part, friend, once forever.
You go ten thousand miles, drifting away
Like an unrooted water-grass.
Oh, the floating clouds and the thoughts of a wanderer!
Oh, the sunset and the longing of an old friend!
We ride away from each other, waving our hands,
While our horses neigh softly, softly...

61. MAID OF WU

Wine of the grapes,
Goblets of gold—
And a pretty maid of Wu—
She comes on pony-back: she is fifteen.
Blue-painted eyebrows—
Shoes of pink brocade—
Inarticulate speech—
But she sings bewitchingly well.
So feasting at the table
Inlaid with tortoise shell,
She gets drunk in my lap.
Ah, child, what caresses
Behind lily-broidered curtains!

62. THE LOTUS

In the deep sequestered stream the lotus grows,
Blooming fresh and fair in the morning sun.
Its glowing petals hide the clear autumn water,
And its thick leaves spread like blue smoke.
Alas! in vain its beauty excels the world.
Who knows? Who will speak of its rare perfume?
Lo, the frost will come, chilling the air,
And its crimson must wither, its fragrance fade.
Ill it has chosen the place to plant its root.
Would it could move to the margin of a flower pond!

An obvious metaphor, reminding one of that flower which "wastes its sweetness in the desert air." Such poems were popular and accorded a high regard by the Chinese scholars, who relish greatly the moral meanings that they themselves read into the simple folk songs in the Book of Odes *compiled by Confucius. Li Po has left us a few scores of these allegorical poems, and it is these that Li Yang-ping in his* Preface *speaks of so highly. See Appendix II.*

63. TO HIS TWO CHILDREN

In the land of Wu the mulberry leaves are green,
And thrice the silkworms have gone to sleep.
In East Luh where my family stay,
I wonder who is sowing those fields of ours.
I cannot be back in time for the spring doings,
Yet I can help nothing, traveling on the river.
The south wind blowing wafts my homesick spirit
And carries it up to the front of our familiar tavern.
There I see a peach tree on the east side of the house
With thick leaves and branches waving in the blue mist.
It is the tree I planted before my parting three years ago.
The peach tree has grown now as tall as the tavern roof,
While I have wandered about without returning.
Ping-yang, my pretty daughter, I see you stand
By the peach tree and pluck a flowering branch.
You pluck the flowers, but I am not there—
How your tears flow like a stream of water!
My little son, Po-chin, grown up to your sister's shoulders,
You come out with her under the peach tree,
But who is there to pat you on the back?
When I think of these things, my senses fail,
And a sharp pain cuts my heart every day.
Now I tear off a piece of white silk to write this letter,
And send it to you with my love a long way up the river.

Written from Nanking during his southern travels prior to his journey to the court of Chang-an. His family lived in East Luh, a central part of Shantung.

64. TO A FRIEND GOING HOME

It is June when the south wind blows the white sand,
And the oxen pant under the moon, their gusty breath turning to mist.
The lowland air is humid and suffocating, and it is hard to bear.
There is no coach on the long road in the burning heat.
What do you think of going by way of the river?
You leave for Chin-ling, hoisting your sail high to the breeze.
Your parents are waiting and watching for you, leaning against the gate.
In Luh-chung there is the home of your childhood.

My family live for the time at the Sand Hill;
I have not returned for three years, and they are distracted.
Please, go and see them!—You know Po-chin, my boy.
He must be running his toy cart and riding on the back of a white sheep.

Written about the same time as No. 63.
The poet is near Chin-ling—that is, Nanking. In this southern region the oxen are so afraid of the scorching sun that they pant, it is said, even at the sight of the moon.
Luh-chung is a district, and Sand Hill a town, in Shantung. See No. 80.

65. A MOUNTAIN REVELRY

To wash and rinse our souls of their age-old sorrows,
We drained a hundred jugs of wine.
A splendid night it was…
In the clear moonlight we were loath to go to bed,
But at last drunkenness overtook us;
And we laid ourselves down on the empty mountain,
The earth for pillow, and the great heaven for coverlet.

66. THE OLD DUST

The living is a passing traveler;
The dead, a man come home.
One brief journey betwixt heaven and earth,
Then, alas! we are the same old dust of ten thousand ages.
The rabbit in the moon pounds the medicine in vain;
Fu-sang, the tree of immortality, has crumbled to kindling wood.
Man dies, his white bones are dumb without a word
When the green pines feel the coming of the spring.
Looking back, I sigh; looking before, I sigh again.
What is there to prize in the life's vaporous glory?

According to Chinese folklore there is a rabbit in the moon, which is pounding the elixir of life.

67. A PAIR OF SWALLOWS

Swallows, two by two,—always two by two.
A pair of swallows are an envy for man.
Such a pair lived together once in a jeweled palace tower.
Long they lived together by the gilded window with silken curtains.

Then fire swept the royal tower.
The swallows entered the Palace of Wu and made their nest.
But once more fire burned the palace down.
Burned away the swallow nest and all the younglings.
Only did the mother bird escape death; she is worn with grief.
Poor lonely swallow, she longs for her mate that is dead.
Never again, can the two fly together.
And that pierces my little heart with sadness.

Another allegorical poem. A commentator says that this is a fable of Li Po's own life, he with his hopes and ambitions being compared with the mother swallow with her mate and younglings. The first palace, then, would allude to the court of Hsuan Tsung; and the second palace to that of the Prince of Yung.

68. AT A RIVER TOWN

A river town. The autumn rain has stopt.
Our wine is gone. So, farewell!
While you lie idle in your boat,
Your sail flies down homeward over the waves,
Past the islands burning red with flowers,
Past the slender willows, green on the river strand.

What of me after parting? I know not—
I'll go back, perhaps, to my old fishing rock on the beach.

69. I AM A PEACH TREE

I am a peach tree blossoming in a deep pit
Who is there I may turn to and smile?
You are the moon up in the far sky;
Passing, you looked down on me an hour; then went on forever.

A sword with the keenest edge,
Could not cut the stream of water in twain
So that it would cease to flow.
My thought is like the stream; and flows and follows you on forever.

These two stanzas are taken from a poem written by Li Po in behalf of his wife, expressing her sentiment toward himself.

70. THE SILK SPINNER

Up the river by the White King City,
The water swells and the wind is high.
It is May. Through the Chu-tang gorge
Who dares to sail down to me now—
Down to Ching-chow, where the barley is ripe
And the silk worms have made their cocoons—
Where I sit and spin, with my thoughts of you
Endless as the silken strands?
The cuckoo calls high up in the air. Ah, me!…

The White King City is in Ssuchuan. The Chu-tang gorge, situated near Wushan in the same province, is one of the most dangerous spots in the Yangtze kiang. Further down the river and in Hupeh, Ching-chow is located, where the silk spinner awaits her lover.

71. CHUANG CHOU AND THE BUTTERFLY

Chuang Chou in dream became a butterfly,
And the butterfly became Chuang Chou at waking.
Which was the real—the butterfly or the man?
Who can tell the end of the endless changes of things?
The water that flows into the depth of the distant sea
Returns anon to the shallows of a transparent stream.
The man, raising melons outside the green gate of the city,
Was once the Prince of the East Hill.
So must rank and riches vanish.
You know it, still you toil and toil,—what for?

Chuang Chou. A famous philosopher of the 3rd and 4th centuries B. C., who was an ardent follower of Laotzu, the founder of Taoism. Chuang Chou's writing contains a chapter on his becoming a butterfly in a dream.

72. THE POET MOURNS HIS JAPANESE FRIEND

Alas, Chao of Nippon—you who left the Imperial City
To sail the waters where the fabled islands are!
Alas, the bright moon has sunk into the blue sea nevermore to return,
And gray clouds of sorrow fill the far skies of the south.

Chao is the Chinese name adopted by a Japanese, Abe Nakamaro, who, on arriving from Japan, was so fascinated with the brilliant court and city of Chang-an, that he chose to remain in China all his life. Once he sailed for home, but his ship encountered a storm and was blown to the south coast of China. At the first report of the mishap his friends at

Chang-an believed that he was dead, and threnodies were composed, of which this poem by Li Po was one.

73. IN THE SPRING-TIME ON THE SOUTH SIDE OF THE YANGTZE KIANG

The green spring—and what time?
The yellow bird sings and will not cease.
On the bank of the Kiang I am growing old, white-haired.
My homeward way lies lost beyond the horizon.
Though my thoughts fly into the clouds of Chin,
I remain with my shadow under the moon of Chu.
My life is a wasted thing,
My garden and fields have long been buried under weeds.
What am I to do so late in my years
But sing away and let alone the imperial gate of gold?

74. THE STEEP ROAD TO SHUH

Alas! how precipitous! Alas! how high!
The road to Shuh is more difficult to climb than to climb the steep blue heaven.
In the remotest time of Tsang-tsung and Yu-fu—
Yea, forty milleniums ago—that land was founded.
Yet from the wall of the Middle Kingdom runs no highway thither, no highway
    linking human dwellings;
Only a lone precipitous path—the bird-way—was built,
Leading westward toward the evening star,
And trailing across the forehead of the Yo-mei mountain.
And how those strong men died, traveling over!
The earth sunk and the mountains crumbled.
At last there is now a road of many ladders and bridges hooked together in the
    air.
Lo, the road-mark high above, where the six dragons circle the sun!
Lo, the stream far below, winding forth and winding back, breaks into foam!
The yellow crane could not fly over these mountaintops;
And the monkeys wail, unable to leap over these gorges.
How the Green Mud path turns round and round!—
There are nine turns to each hundred steps.
The traveler must climb into the very realm of stars, and gasp for breath;
Then draw a long sigh, his hands on his breast.

Oh, why go you west, I pray? And when will you return?
I fear for you. You cannot clamber over these jutting rocks.
You shall see nothing by day but the birds plaining bitterly on the aged trees, the
    female following the male in their flight;
You shall hear no voice but the cuckoos calling in the moonlight by night,
    calling mournfully in the desolate mountains.
The road to Shuh is more difficult to climb than to climb the steep blue heaven.
A mere story of it makes the youth's red face grow pale.

The lofty peaks shoot up cloudward in rows. If one foot higher, they would touch the heaven.

The dead pine trees cling to the cliff, hanging headmost over the abyss.

The sparkling cascades and the spurting torrents vie with one another to make the bellowing din.

Anon, a giant boulder tumbles from the crag-head; a thousand mountain walls resound like thunder.

O you wayfarers from afar, why do you come hither on this direful road?
The gate of the Sword Parapet stands firm on its frightful height.
One man defending it, a thousand men could not break it open.
And the keepers of the gate are not of your kin,
They may turn, I fear, to wolves and leopards.
Fleeing at morn before the savage tigers,
Fleeing at eve before the huge serpents,
Men are killed and cut up like hemp,
While the beasts whet their fangs and lick the blood.
Though many pleasures there may be in the brocade city of Shuh,
It were better to return to your house quickly.
The road to Shuh is more difficult to climb than to climb the steep blue heaven.
I shrug my shoulders and heave a long sigh—gazing into the west.

This is one of the most admired and most difficult poems of Li Po, certain portions of it being as vague as they are beautiful. Some commentators maintain that this was written at the time of the An Lu-shan rebellion, when the emperor Hsuan Tsung fled to Ssuchuan, to which course Li Po was opposed; but being in no position to declare his opinion openly, the poet voiced it thus in verse covertly. The poem hints at the double danger for the emperor in leaving his capital to the rebels who are tigers and serpents as well as in trusting his person to the hands of the strangers of Shuh, who might turn to wolves and leopards, while it dwells for the most part on the difficulty of the journey in a remarkably vivid and forceful language. The Road to Shuh runs from Shensi to Ssuchuan over the mountains.

As to those "strong men" that died, there is this story: Some thousands of years ago, a prince in Shensi, knowing the fondness of the king of Shuh, offered him his five daughters for wives. The king of Shuh despatched five strong men to fetch the princesses. It was on their homeward journey that the party saw a big serpent crawling into a hole in the mountainside. One man tried to pull out the serpent by its tail, but could not do so. All the five men joined in the enterprise, and yelling aloud, they pulled the serpent, whereupon the whole mountain range crumbled and was split into five peaks. The five strong men and the five princesses and all the attendants perished.

75. PARTING AT A TAVERN OF CHIN-LING

The wind blows the willow bloom and fills the whole tavern with fragrance
While the pretty girls of Wu bid us taste the new wine.
My good comrades of Chin-ling, hither you have come to see me off.
I, going, still tarry; and we drain our cups evermore.
Pray ask the river, which is the longer of the two—
Its east-flowing stream, or the thoughts of ours at parting!

76. THE PHOENIX BIRD TOWER

Here once on the Phoenix Bird Tower the phoenix birds came to nest.
Now the birds are gone, and the tower empty; only the river flows aimlessly on.
Here where the garden of Wu palace bloomed, the deep grass hides the paths;
Where the kings of Chin vaunted their regalia, is only an old hill.
I see the three peaks hang aloft as though half-dropt from the sky,
And the river divide in two streams, holding the White Heron Island between.
But the floating clouds cover the sun,
And the city of Chang-an is lost in distance and gloom.

The Phoenix Bird Tower was situated to the north of Nanking, once the capital of Wu, Chin, and many other states. A legend has it that three birds of five-colored wings, resembling the peacock, nestled here once, and they sang so melodiously that all other birds of the vicinity were attracted to the tower. Those three birds were the Phoenix.

77. HIS DREAM OF THE SKY-LAND: A FAREWELL POEM

The sea-farers tell of the Eastern Isle of Bliss,
It is lost in a wilderness of misty sea waves.

But the Sky-land of the south, the Yueh-landers say,
May be seen through cracks of the glimmering cloud.

This land of the sky stretches across the leagues of heaven;
It rises above the Five Mountains and towers over the Scarlet Castle,
While, as if staggering before it, the Tien-tai Peak
Of forty-eight thousand feet leans toward the southeast.

So, longing to dream of the southlands of Wu and Yueh,
I flew across the Mirror Lake one night under the moon.

The moon in the lake followed my flight,
Followed me to the town of Yen-chi.
Here still stands the mansion of Prince Hsieh.
I saw the green waters curl and heard the monkeys' shrill cries.
I climbed, putting on the clogs of the prince,
Skyward on a ladder of clouds,

And half-way up from the sky-wall I saw the morning sun,
And heard the heaven's cock crowing in the mid-air.
Now among a thousand precipices my way wound round and round;
Flowers choked the path; I leaned against a rock; I swooned.

Roaring bears and howling dragons roused me—Oh, the clamorous waters of the
    rapids!
I trembled in the deep forest, and shuddered at the overhanging crags, one
    heaped upon another.
Clouds on clouds gathered above, threatening rain;
The waters gushed below, breaking into mist.

A peal of blasting thunder!
The mountains crumbled.
The stone gate of the hollow heaven
Opened wide, revealing
A vasty realm of azure without bottom,
Sun and moon shining together on gold and silver palaces.

Clad in rainbow and riding on the wind,
The ladies of the air descended like flower-flakes;
The faery lords trooping in, they were thick as hempstalks in the fields.

Phoenix birds circled their cars, and panthers played upon harps.
Bewilderment filled me, and terror seized on my heart.
I lifted myself in amazement, and alas!
I woke and found my bed and pillow—
Gone was the radiant world of gossamer.

So with all pleasures of life.
All things pass with the east-flowing water.
I leave you and go—when shall I return?
Let the white roe feed at will among the green crags,
Let me ride and visit the lovely mountains!
How can I stoop obsequiously and serve the mighty ones!
It stifles my soul.

In this poem the poet describes his dream of visiting Mt. Tien-mu, "Fostermother of the shies," in Chehkiang. The other mountains, Chi-Cheng, the "Scarlet Castle," and Tien-tai, the "Terrace of Heaven" are located in the same province.
Prince Hsieh is the one poet-governor mentioned in 35.

78. IN MEMORIAM

(The poet mourns Ho Chi-chang)

Ssu-ming had a man of madness,
Ho Chi-chang, frenzied with wind and stream.
The first time I met him at Chang-an,
He called me "a god in exile."
O dear lover of the cup,
He has turned the sod under the pine tree—
He who bartered his gold turtle for wine.
Now, alone, I shed tears, remembering him.

Ho Chi-chang. The jovial courtier who introduced Li Po to Hsuan Tsung. Ssu-ming, a district in Chehkiang, was his ancestral home, to which he retired and where he died. See the Introduction, also No. 125.

The gold turtle was probably a trinket of some sort, worn as an ornament.

79. ON THE ROAD OF AMBITION

(The poet departs from Nan-ling for the capital)

Home in the mountains in autumn-tide
Of new-brewed wine and yellow chick fattened on grain.
I call the boy to boil the fowl and pour the white wine,
While my children, playing noisily about, tug me by the sleeve.
I sing and imbibe the bland ecstasy of the cup;
I rise and dance in the tangled beams of the setting sun.

It is not too late to win a lord of ten thousand chariots.
Let me ride and spur my horse on the long, long road!

The silly woman of Kuei-chi may scorn Chu Mai-chen,
I take leave of my family and journey west to Chin.
Looking up at the sky, I laugh aloud and go.
Ha, am I one to crawl ever in the dust-laden weeds?

Chu Mai-chen. Died B. C. 116. A wood-cutter under the Han dynasty, whose wife left him because she could not endure poverty. By diligent study, however, he became governor of Kuei-chi in Chehkiang; and his wife, who had sunk to destitution, begged to be allowed to rejoin him. But he replied, "If you can pick up spilt water, you may return"; whereupon his wife went and hanged herself—Giles: Biographical Dictionary No. 65.

It is quite likely that the poet by the "silly woman of Kuei-chi" alludes to his own wife, who had left him because of his poor success in life.

80. TO TU FU FROM SAND HILL CITY

Why have I come hither, after all?
Solitude is my lot at Sand Hill City.
There are old trees by the city wall,
And busy voices of autumn, day and night.
The Luh wine will not soothe my soul,
Nor the touching songs of Chi move me;
But all my thoughts flow on to you
With the waters of the Min endlessly southward.

81. A VINDICATION

If heaven loved not the wine,
A Wine Star would not be in heaven;
If earth loved not the wine,
The Wine Spring would not be on the earth.
Since heaven and earth love the wine,
Need a tippling mortal be ashamed?
The transparent wine, I hear,
Has the soothing virtue of a sage,
While the turgid is rich, they say,
As the fertile mind of the wise.
Both the sage and the wise were drinkers,
Why seek for peers among gods and goblins?
Three cups open the grand door to bliss;
Take a jugful, the universe is yours.
Such is the rapture of the wine,
That the sober shall never inherit.

82. TO LUH, THE REGISTRAR

It is autumn near and far.
Outside the gate all the hills are barren.
A white cloud, my old friend,
Beckons me from far empyreal space.
Pray, when will Luh Chen-ho come back—
He who has flown west like a crane?

A native commentator remarks: "This poem would be better if the last two lines and the title were left out."

83. TO THE FISHERMAN

Shake not your crown, if perfumed;
Nor flap your garment, if spiced with *lan*!
It is better to hide the chaste soul's radiance,
The world hates a thing too pure.

There goes the fisherman of Tsang-lang.
Await me, old man, I will go with you.

84. THE TEARS OF BANISHMENT

The flow-tide ebbs back to sea.
My friend returned to Wu from banishment.
I asked him about the sorrows of exile.
His tears fell like pearls of the South Sea.

85. THE LOTUS GATHERER

On the river margin of Jo-yeh she is gathering the lotus;
She talks to her companions and laughs among the lilies.
The clear sunlit water reflects her gay attire,
And her perfumed sleeves flap lightly in the wind.

But who are these cavaliers on the bank?
By twos, by threes, they glint through the drooping willows;
Their horses neigh among the blown flowers, and are gone.
She sees and lingers with an anguish in her heart.

The Jo-yeh River is in Chehkiang, and flows into Ching Hu, or the Mirror Lake.

86. THE SPORT-FELLOWS

You had a yellow steed,
Mine was white.
Their colors differed,
Our hearts were one.

We two gay blades of Lo-yang,
Rode the city street, side by side,
Flaunting our high head-gears gallantly,
Our long swords glancing in the sun.
Each had a fur coat on, worth a thousand guilders;
Both were guests of the five princes.

Now you have fallen as a tiger falls in a trap-hole;
And suffer miserably as strong men must sometimes.
But when you, my comrade, are so distressed,
What avails me if I alone can flourish?

87. THE DANCING GIRL

With her limpid voice,
Her pearly teeth revealing,
The northern maid, the prettiest child,
Sings "Downy grasses," instead of "Blue water."
Then, brushing her face with her long sleeve, she rises for your sake.

She dances like the winter-cloud that curls over the frothy sea;
She dances like the wild fowl of Tartary, wind-blown toward the sky.

The kingly hall is full of radiant faces; the pleasure will not end.
With sundown the flute sounds thicken, and the mellow voices of the singing
    girls.

88. THE ROVER OF CHAO

Oh, the Rover of Chao with his Tartar-fashioned cap,
A scimitar on his side, gleaming bright like the snow,
The silver saddle glittering on his white horse,
Behold, he comes and is gone like a shooting star;

Kills a man at every ten paces as he goes,
And goes he a thousand miles without stopping.
The deed done, he shakes his raiment and departs—
None knows whither, nor even his name.

He stops at leisure and drinks with Prince Hsin-ling,
Laying his drawn sword across his knee;
Picks up a piece of roast meat for Chu-hai to eat;
Offers a goblet of wine to Hou-ying to drink;

After three rounds gives a pledge of fealty,
And weightier is his vow even than the Five Mountains.
When his ears are hot and his eyes burn,
His heroic soul blazes forth like a rainbow.

A hammer in his hand saved the kingdom of Chao,
And the whole city of Han-tan shook with terror.
How the glory of two such strong men shines
For a thousand autumns over the ramparts of Tai-Liang!

Sweet honor perfumes their heroic bones,
Putting to shame the literati of the world,
Who can only recline in the study
And whiten their heads over books like the Tai-hsuan Ching.

Wu Chi was the name of Prince Hsin-ling of the Wei state in the 3rd century B. C.
Hou Ying was a recluse through whom Prince Hsin-ling obtained the service of Chu Hai, who was a rover of the type depicted in the present poem. When the state of Chao was attacked by a hostile state and its capital Han-tan was beleaguered, Hsin-ling and Chu Hai went to the rescue. Chu Hai—a very strong man—brained an irresolute general with a heavy hammer, while, by taking command of his army, Hsin-ling raised the siege of Han-tan.
Tai-liang was the capital of the State of Wei.
Tai-hsuan Ching. A learned book written by Yang Hsiung (B. C. 53-A. D. 18).

89. TO HIS FRIEND AT CHIANG-HSIA

When the brazen Tartars came with their frightened horses kicking up dust and
    sand,
While the Tartar horde watered their horses in the Tien-chin River,
You, governor of Chang-yeh, then, resided near Wine Spring;
I, banished nine thousand *li*, was in the land of Pa.

When the world was put to order, and the laws made lenient,
I, an Yeh-lang exile, stricken with the chilly frost,
How I longed for my friend in the west whom I could
Only the east wind bore my dream back to Chang-an.

What a chance that I met you in this place!
In joy and bewilderment I felt like one fallen from the cloud.
And amid the noise of pipes and flutes at the joyous feast
I endeavored in vain to utter long sentences.

Yesterday, clad in a brocade robe, I poured the costly wine.
To-day, sore-afflicted, I am dumb like the speechless trees.
Once I rode on horseback in the great imperial park;
Now I jog about slowly from house to house of mandarins.

At Nan-ping I met the governor and opened my heart;
Now with you I may hold sweet conversation.
Even as the leagues of cloud melt above the mountain,
Opening the view of the blue sky around, so melts my grief.

Oh, grief! Oh, bitter pain, and pain evermore!
Sorrowing, I drink two thousand jugs of wine—
The cold ashes are warm again, and the spring is born.
And you, jolly wise host without compare,
Drunken, you go about, riding on the back of a mule.

In the cloister yonder under clouds and the moon there are monks galore.
But the mountains and waters—did they ever cater to man's desires?
Ah, no! Better blow your reed pipes, beat your drums, and wanton on the river
    water.
Call forth the young girls of the south and bid them sing the boat songs!

I will knock down the Yellow Crane House for you with a hammer,
You may upset the Parrot Island, too, for my sake.
The heroic battle of the Red Walls was fought as in a dream—
Let me sing and dance and lighten the sorrow of separation!

90. THE CATARACT OF LUH SHAN—I

Westward I ascend the Peak of Incense Burner;
Southward I see the mighty waterfall.
It plunges three hundred *chang* down the mountain,
And froths for miles in the rapids below.
As wind-driven snow speed the waters,
Like a white rainbow spanning the dark.
I wonder if Heaven's River had fallen from above
To course through the mid-sky of clouds,
Long I lift my gaze—Oh, prodigious force!
How majestic the creation of gods!
Unwavering before the ocean winds that blow,
Glaring at the faint moon from over the river,
Profusely it sprays the sky
And drenches the green mountain walls.
The swift torrents boil over giant rocks;
The flying water scatters a mist of ethereal gems.

O mountains of renown that I adore,
You fill my heart with deep repose.
No longer need I take the potion of precious stones,
You can wash away the earth stains from my face.
Let me be with the things I love,
And leave the world of man forever.

91. THE CATARACT OF LUH SHAN—II

The sun shines on the Peak of Incense Burner,
And the purple vapor rises like smoke.
Lo, the long stream of water hung up yonder!
Straight down three thousand *chi* the flying torrent leaps,
As if the Silver River were falling from the ninth heaven.

The Silver River, i. e., The Milky Way.

92. BEREFT OF THEIR LOVE

Bereft of their love,
Huang and Yin, the royal ladies of old,
Ranged the banks of Hsiao and Hsiang, south of Tung-ting.
They wandered by the fathomless waters of the deep.
All the world tells the tale of their misery.

Dark is the day, and dismal the clouds;
Demons howl in the fog and infernal spirits whistle in the rain.
Ah, me! What would it avail me if I dared to speak?
High heaven shines not, I fear, on the loyalty of my heart.
Clouds gather clouds,—they would roar aloud in anger.
Even Yao and Shun ruling, the scepter would pass to Yui.
A king, deprived of his minister, is a dragon turned to a fish;
A minister usurps power, lo! a mouse is become a tiger.

Yao was imprisoned, they say, and Shun died in the open field.
The Nine Hills of Perplexity stand in a row, one resembling another—
How could they find the solitary mound of the Double pupiled One?

The king's daughters cried where the black clouds lowered;
Their lord was gone like wind and wave never to return.
They wept and moaned, and gazed into the distance.
Gazed longingly toward the deep mountains of Tsang-wu.

The Mountains of Tsang-wu may crumble, the River Hsiang go dry.
Their tears on the bamboo leaves will not fade forever.

Huang and Hu Yin (24th century B. C.) were two daughters of Emperor Tao, who gave them in marriage to his successor, Shun—the Double-pupiled One. Shun, while traveling south in the district of Tsang-wu (Hunan Province) died and was buried in the field. The two wives arrived too late to meet their husband, and their tear-marks produced a new species of bamboo with speckled leaves. Yui succeeded Shun as emperor.

The original of this poem, much prized for its verbal beauty and its classic allegory, is quite obscure. The native commentators have a great deal to say on the significance of the second stanza. At any rate, it is clear that Li Po, while retelling the well-known legend, alludes to his separation from the emperor and to the unhappy state of affairs at the court that was infested with unworthy and wicked men.

93. LADY WANG-CHAO—I

Lady Chao brushes the saddle inlaid with pearl;
She mounts her palfrey and weeps,
Wetting her rose-red cheeks with tears.
To-day a high-born lady in the palace of Han,
To-morrow in a far land
She will be a barbarian slave.

Lady Wang-chao, a lady in the seraglio of the emperor Yuan-ti of the Han dynasty, was one of the early victims of the political marriages, which the ruling house of China was compelled to make from time to time with the chieftains of the barbarian tribes in order to avoid their savage incursions into the Middle Flower Kingdom.

This emperor had so many beauties, it is said, that for the sake of convenience he ordered their portraits to be painted. All the ladies bribed the artist, except Lady Wang-chao, who was consequently very unfavorably represented in the private gallery of the sovereign. So when a lady of the palace had to be presented to a Tartar chieftain, the emperor chose Wang-chao, believing her to be the easiest one to spare. He discovered his mistake too late. She died in the barbarian land; singularly enough, over her little mound in the desert the grass, they say, was always green.

94. LADY WANG-CHAO—II

The moon above the palace of Han
    And above the land of Chin,
Shedding a flood of silvery light,
    Bids the radiant lady farewell.
She sets out on the road of the Jewel Gate—
    The road she will not travel back.
The moon returns above the palace of Han,
    Rising from the eastern seas,
But the radiant lady wed in the west,
    She will return nevermore.
On the Mongolian mountains flowers are made
    Of the long winter's snow.
The moth-eyebrowed one, broken-hearted,
    Lies buried in the desert sand.
Living, she lacked the gold,
    And her portrait was distorted;
Dying she leaves a green mound,
    Which moves all the world to pity.

95. THE NORTH WIND

The lamp-bearing dragon nestles over the polar gate,
And his light illumines the frigid zone.
For neither the sun nor the moon shines there,
But only the north wind comes, blowing and howling from heaven.
The snow-flakes of the Yen mountains are big like pillows,
They are blown down, myriads together, over the Hsuan-yuan palace.

'Tis December. Lo, the pensive maid of Yu-chow!
She will not sing, she will not smile; her moth-eyebrows are disheveled.
She stands by the gate and watches the wayfarers pass,
Remembering him who snatched his sword and went to save the borderland,
Him who suffered bitterly in the cold beyond the Great Wall,
Him who fell in the battle and will never come back.

In the tiger-striped gold case he left for her keeping
There remains a pair of white-feathered arrows
Amid the cobwebs and dust gathered of long years—
Oh, empty tokens of love, too sad to look upon!
She takes them out and burns them to ashes.
By building a dam one may stop the flow of the Yellow River,
But who can assuage the grief of her heart when it snows and the north wind
　　blows?

96. THE BORDERLAND MOON

The bright moon is above the Peak of Heaven
In the far cloud-sea of Tartary.

The wind sweeps on for ten thousand miles
And blows over the Pass of the Jewel Gate.

The imperial army marches down the Po-tung road
While the barbarian foe pries the Bay of Chin-hai.

The warriors watch the skies of the borderland,
And many faces are sad with thoughts of home.

Never yet from the battlefield
A man was seen returning—alas!

To-night at the high house, where she is waiting,
There is sighing and moaning without ceasing.

The Jewel Gate Pass, or Yu-men, in Anhsi, Kansu.
Po-tung. Perhaps, Ba-tung, on the old trade route to Tibet.
Ching-hai. Kokonor, a lake in Mongolia.

97. THE NEFARIOUS WAR

Last year we fought by the head-stream of the So-kan,
This year we are righting on the Tsung-ho road.
We have washed our armor in the waves of the Chiao-chi lake,
We have pastured our horses on Tien-shan's snowy slopes.
The long, long war goes on ten thousand miles from home,
Our three armies are worn and grown old.

The barbarian does man-slaughter for plowing;
On his yellow sand-plains nothing has been seen but blanched skulls and bones.
Where the Chin emperor built the walls against the Tartars,
There the defenders of Han are burning beacon fires.
The beacon fires burn and never go out,
There is no end to war!—

In the battlefield men grapple each other and die;
The horses of the vanquished utter lamentable cries to heaven,
While ravens and kites peck at human entrails,
Carry them up in their flight, and hang them on the branches of dead trees.

So, men are scattered and smeared over the desert grass,
And the generals have accomplished nothing.

Oh, nefarious war! I see why arms
Were so seldom used by the benign sovereigns.

98. BEFORE THE CASK OF WINE

The spring wind comes from the east and quickly passes,
Leaving faint ripples in the wine of the golden bowl.
The flowers fall, flake after flake, myriads together.

      You, pretty girl, wine-flushed,
      Your rosy face is rosier still.
      How long may the peach and plum trees flower
      By the green-painted house?
      The fleeting light deceives man,
      Brings soon the stumbling age.

Rise and dance
In the westering sun,
While the urge of youthful years is yet unsubdued!
What avails to lament after one's hair has turned white like silken threads?

99. YUAN TAN-CHIU OF THE EAST MOUNTAIN

You, the dweller of the East Mountain,
You, the lover of the beauty of hills and valleys,
In the green spring you sleep in the empty woodland,
And hardly rise in the broad daylight.
The pine wind shakes your garment,
And the stony brook cleanses your soul.
How I envy you, who, unperturbed,
Are pillowed high in a mist of emerald!

100. LINES

Cool is the autumn wind,
Clear the autumn moon,
The blown leaves heap up and scatter again;
A raven, cold-stricken, starts from his roost.
Where are you, beloved?—When shall I see you once more?
Ah, how my heart aches to-night—this hour!

101. THE BALLADS OF THE FOUR SEASONS: SPRING

The lovely Lo-foh of the land of Chin,
Is plucking mulberry leaves by the blue water.
On the green boughs her white arms gleam,
And the bright sun shines upon her scarlet dress.
"My silk-worms," says she, "are hungry, I must go.
"Tarry not with your five horses, Prince, I pray!"

Lo-foh is the heroine of a popular ballad, which was already old at Li Po's time, and which served as the basis of the present poem. The original, much longer and charmingly naive, runs as follows:

The sun rises from the southeast nook.
It shines on the house of Master Chin.
Master Chin, he has a comely daughter.
Lo-foh is her name.

Lo-foh feeds her silk-worms well.
She picks mulberry leaves south of the city.
Her basket has a cord of blue silk;
And a hook made of a laurel branch.

Her hair is dressed in pretty knots of Wa-do;
Bright moonstones hang from her ears.
Of yellow silk is her petticoat,
And of purple silk her jacket.

The Lord Governor, he comes from the south,
His five horses stop and stay.
The Lord Governor bids his men ask;
And they say: "Who art thou, little maid?"

"I am the fair daughter of Master Chin,
"Lo-foh is my name."
"How old art thou, Lo-foh?"
"I am still less than twenty,
"But more than fifteen—yea, much more."

The Lord Governor, he entreats Lo-foh.
Says he, "Wilt thou ride with me, yea or nay?"
Lo-foh comes forward and replies:
"My Lord Governor," says she, "how foolish, indeed!
"My Lord Governor, you have your own lady,
"And Lo-foh, she has a man of her own."

102. THE BALLADS OF THE FOUR SEASONS: SUMMER

On the Mirror Lake three hundred *li* around
Gaily the lotus lilies bloom.
She gathers them—Queen Hsi-shih, in Maytime!
A multitude jostles on the bank, watching.
Her boat turns back without waiting the moonrise,
And glides away to the house of the amorous Yueh king.

Queen Hsi-shih. See Note under No. 43.

103. THE BALLADS OF THE FOUR SEASONS: AUTUMN

The moon is above the city of Chang-an,
From ten thousand houses comes the sound of cloth pounding;
The sad autumn wind blows, and there is no end
To my thought of you beyond the Jewel Gate Pass.
When will the barbarian foe be vanquished,
And you, my beloved, return from the far battlefield?

Cloth-pounding is the ironing part in the old-fashioned Chinese laundering process.
On account of the hardness of the wooden stand and mallet employed for it, the pounding
produces a shrill metallic sound. Women working late, and their mallets clanging
through the night, have long been a popular theme for poets.

In the present poem the situation is pathetic since from the ten thousand houses,
where women are working late in the night, men have gone to the far battle front.
The Jewel Gate Pass, is located at the western extremity of Kansu province.

104. THE BALLADS OF THE FOUR SEASONS: WINTER

The courier will depart on the morrow for the front.
All night she sews a soldier's jacket.
Her fingers, plying the needle, are numb with cold;
Scarce can she hold the icy scissors.
At last the work is done; she sends it a long, long way,
Oh, how many days before it reaches him in Lin-tao?

Lin-tao, a town on the frontier of Tu-fan, whose warlike tribes had harassed the
Chinese empire for centuries past.

105. TWO LETTERS FROM CHANG-KAN—I

(A river-merchant's wife writes)

I would play, plucking flowers by the gate;
My hair scarcely covered my forehead, then.
You would come, riding on your bamboo horse,
And loiter about the bench with green plums for toys.
So we both dwelt in Chang-kan town,
We were two children, suspecting nothing.

At fourteen I became your wife,
And so bashful that I could never bare my face,
But hung my head, and turned to the dark wall;
You would call me a thousand times,
But I could not look back even once.

At fifteen I was able to compose my eyebrows,
And beg you to love me till we were dust and ashes.
You always kept the faith of Wei-sheng,
Who waited under the bridge, unafraid of death,
I never knew I was to climb the Hill of Wang-fu
And watch for you these many days.

I was sixteen when you went on a long journey,
Traveling beyond the Keu-Tang Gorge,
Where the giant rocks heap up the swift river,
And the rapids are not passable in May.
Did you hear the monkeys wailing
Up on the skyey height of the crags?
Do you know your foot-marks by our gate are old,
And each and every one is filled up with green moss?

The mosses are too deep for me to sweep away;
And already in the autumn wind the leaves are falling.
The yellow butterflies of October
Flutter in pairs over the grass of the west garden.
My heart aches at seeing them...
I sit sorrowing alone, and alas!
The vermilion of my face is fading.

Some day when you return down the river,
If you will write me a letter beforehand,
I will come to meet you—the way is not long—
I will come as far as the Long Wind Beach instantly.

Chang-kan is a suburb of Nanking.

The Long Wind Beach, or Chang-feng Sha, is in Anhwei, several hundred miles up the river, from Nanking. It is really a long way. But by making the wife say that the way is not long, Li Po brings out the girlishness of the speaker.

Wang-fu means "husband watching" and more than one hill has taken that name because of a similar tradition of a forlorn wife who climbed the height to watch for the return of her husband.

Wei Sheng. 6th century B. C. He was a young man of fidelity. He promised to meet a girl under a bridge in Chang-an, and waited for her there. Though the girl did not appear and the river water was rising, he would not leave his post and was drowned.

106. TWO LETTERS FROM CHANG-KAN—II

(Another river-merchant's wife writes)

I lived in my maiden bower,
Unaware of all things of the world.
Since married to you of Chang-kan town,
I wander the river bank to spy the weather.
In May the south wind blows,
I think of you sailing down to Pa-ling;
In August the west wind arises,
And I know you will part from Yangtzu.
You come and go, I sorrow ever,
Seeing you so little, and living so much apart.
When will you arrive at Hsiang-tan?
My dream goes over the wind-tossed waves.
Last night a storm went past in fury,
Tearing down trees on the riverside,
Spreading darkness without end—
Where were you, then, poor traveler?
Would I could ride the swift-drifting cloud,
And meet you in good time east of Orchid Beach!

Oh, the happy pair of mandarin-ducks among the reed,
And the purple kingfishers, embroidered on the gold screen!
Why at fifteen years and little more,
My face pink like the peach flower,
Have I become a river merchant's wife,
To grieve over winds and grieve again over waves!

Pa-ling, is another name for Yo-chow, Hunan.
Hsiang-tan, in Chang-sha fu, Hunan.

107. ON ASCENDING THE SIN-PING TOWER

An exile, I ascend this tower,
Thinking of home, and with the anguish of the waning year.
The sun has set far beyond heaven's immensity;
The unsullied waters flow on in bleak undulation.
I see a stray cloud of Chin above the mountain trees,
And the wild geese of Tartary flying over the river dunes.
Alas! for ten thousand miles under the dark blue sky
As far as my eyes can reach, there is but one vast gloom for me.

Both the stray cloud and the migratory birds remind the poet of his own wanderings.

108. ON GOING TO VISIT A TAOIST RECLUSE ON MOUNT TAI-TIEN, BUT FAILING TO MEET HIM

A dog barks afar where the waters croon.
The peach flowers are deeper-tinted, wet with rain.
The wood is so thick that one espies a deer at times,
But cannot hear the noon bell in this lonely glen.
The wild bamboos sway in the blue mist,
And on the green mountainside flying cascades glisten
What way has he gone? There is none to tell;
Sadly I lean against a pine tree here and there.

Mount Tai-tien is where Li Po used to live, and is known also as the Tai-kuang Mountain. Tu Fu mentions it in one of his poems addressed to Li Po. See No. 127.
"So to your old place of reading in Mount Kuang."

109. AT THE CELL OF AN ABSENT MOUNTAIN PRIEST

By a stony wall I enter the Red Valley.
The pine-tree gate is choked up with green moss;
There are bird-marks on the deserted steps,
But none to open the door of the priest's cell.
I peer through the window and see his white brush
Hung on the wall and covered with dust.
Disappointed, I sigh in vain;

I would go, but loiter wistfully about.
Sweet scented clouds are wafted along the mountainside,
And a rain of flowers falls from the sky.
Here I may taste the bliss of solitude
And listen to the plaint of blue monkeys.
Ah, what tranquility reigns over this ground!
What isolation from all things of the world!

The white brush is carried by the priest as a symbol of purity and cleanliness.

110. ON A MOONLIGHT NIGHT

The stream reflects the lean foliage of a pine—
An old pine of unremembered years.
The cold moonlight gleams on the tremulous water,
And pours into my room by the window door.
I prolong my futile singing to-night,
Deploring thee—how deeply, O prince!
For no more shalt thou see a true vassal like An-tao.
My song, ceasing, leaves the grief in my heart.

This is a poem composed probably after the rebellion of An Lu-shan and the flight of the emperor from the capital, the "prince" referring to the emperor.

111. A VISIT TO YUAN TAN-CHIU IN THE MOUNTAINS

Forth to sylvan retreats I went, a vagabond,
Led by pleasure, and of the distance unaware.
The blue range yonder lay too far to travel
When the giddy sun was ready to set.
Barely had I crossed three, four hills;
The road had taken a thousand and ten thousand turns.

I heard the monkeys wail in the still twilight,
And saw the clouds roll away one by one.
Now came the dainty moon over the tall pines,
How exquisite the autumnal scene of a hollow glen!
There was old snow left in the deep ravine,
And the frosty rapids flew, cutting through rock.

Mountains thrust their peaks in the mid-sky;
I could have climbed and gazed forever
When Tan-chiu, my friend, called me from afar.
He looked at me and burst into laughter.

I went to his hermitage down the valley
And entered the solitude of a recluse.
Here we delighted ourselves night-long—

It was lucid day-break when I spoke of going.

112. A MIDNIGHT FAREWELL

By a pale lantern—under the cold moon
We were drinking heavily together.
Frightened by our orgies, a white heron
Flaffed out of the river shallows. It was midnight.

113. THE SONG OF LUH SHAN

Really I am a mad man of Chu,
Singing the phoenix-bird song and laughing at the sage Confucius.
At dawn a green jade staff in my hand,
I leave the Yellow Crane House and go,
Seeking genii among the Five Mountains, forgetting the distance.
All my life I've loved to visit the mountains of renown.

The Luh Shan looms near the constellation of the South Dipper,
Like a nine-fold screen adorned with embroidery of clouds;
And the clear lake reflects its gleaming emerald.
The two peaks shoot up high where the Gold Gate opens wide;
And over against the far waterfall of the Censer Mountain
The cascades of San-shi-liang hang like the Silver River of heaven.
The craggy ranges over-reach the azure blue;
And girdled in pink mist and green foliage,
They glisten in the morning sun.
The birds cannot fly over—to the remote skies of Wu.
I ascend the high place and look out on heaven and earth.
Lo! the waters of the great Kiang flow on and on never to return.
Anon, blowing yellow clouds miles upon miles, the wind arises,
And through the nine provinces white billows roll on like mountains of snow.

I love to make the song of Luh Shan.
Luh Shan is my joy and inspiration.
I gaze idly into the Stone Mirror to cleanse my soul,
Though the path Prince Shieh went is lost under deep green moss.
I've swallowed early the sacred pellet and forsaken all worldly desires.
Playing on the harp thrice over, I've attained the Way.
I see genii amid the iridescent clouds afar,
Going up to the celestial city with lotus in their hands.
I shall meet the Illimitable above the ninth heaven,
Then, with Lu-ao I hope to journey to the Great Void.

Luh Shan is a mountain near Kiu-kiang, Kiangsi.
When Confucius was visiting the land of Chu, a mad man named Tsu Yu passed him by, laughing and singing, "O phoenix bird, O phoenix bird!" etc. The sage attempted in vain to have an interview with him.

The last stanza refers to the poet's Taoistic attainment and visions.

114. TO HIS WIFE ON HIS DEPARTURE—I

Thrice my prince has called. I shall go, and not return.
To-morrow morn I take leave of you,
And cross the pass of Wu Kuan.
In vain you shall look for me in the white jade house,
But you must go and climb the Hill of Wang-fu longingly.

These three poems were written in 755 when he was setting out to join Li Ling, the prince of Yung.
As to the significance of the Hill of Wang-fu, see the note under No. 105. There was a hill by that name near Hsuan-cheng, Anhwei.

115. TO HIS WIFE ON HIS DEPARTURE—II

At the gate you still hold me by the robe,
And ask me when I shall come back from the west.
I will return some day, wearing, perhaps, a seal of gold.
And you will not imitate the wife of Su Chin,
Who came not down from her loom.

Su Chin (died B. C. 317) was a native of Lo-yang. In his youthful years he went out, seeking for a career, but returned in rags and tatters. His wife would not take the trouble of leaving her place at the loom in order to greet him. However, he succeeded later in his scheme of the federation of six weaker states against the strong state of Chin, and he was appointed prime minister of each of the six states thus combined. A seal of gold was given to a state minister as the symbol of authority.
In this poem Li Po's political ambition is evident.

116. TO HIS WIFE ON HIS DEPARTURE—III

Gold are the staircases, and like a kingfisher's wings
Sparkle the towers of the house where I shall be.
But the thought of you, my dear, who will stand alone.
By the ancient gate and weep,
Will make me sit awake at night by the lonely lamp,
And watch the dying moon of dawn;
And all my tears shall flow as I journey on to the west.

117. ON HIS WHITE HAIR

On the face of the bright mirror, I wonder,
Whence has come this hoar frost of autumn!
Ah, my long, long white hair of three thousand *chang*,
Grown so long with the cares of this world!

Chang is a Chinese unit of measure equal, perhaps, to ten feet. White hair 30,000 feet is certainly long. But this is not ludicrous to Chinese taste, for it is not a foolish extravagance but an innocent form of poetic indulgence.

In Chinese literature figures such as one thousand, three thousands, and ten thousands, simply denote a large number. So we read constantly of a party of ten thousand guests, a waterfall three thousand feet high, and a man emptying one thousand jugfuls of wine.

118. TO THE HONORABLE JUSTICE HSIN

Once we dwelt in the city of Chang-an
In wild ecstasy of flowers and willow-green.
We drank our wine from the same bowls
With five princes and seven dukes.
Our hearts rose and grew blither,
Unflinching in the presence of a warrior lord;
Nor did we fall behind any one, when,
Delighting in wind and stream, we sought beauty.

You had red cheeks, then; and I was young, too.
We sped our horses to Chang-tai's pleasure mart,
And lightly carried our crops of gold;
Offered our essays in the court examination;
And sat feasting at a tortoise table;
And there was endless singing and dancing;...
We thought it would last forever, you and I—
How were we to know that the grass would tremble
And the wind and dust come, roaring down?

Down through the Han-ku Pass
The Tartar horsemen came.
I am an exile now, traveling heavy-hearted,
Far away to the land of Yeh-lang.
The peach and plum trees by the palace
Are opening their petals toward the light—
Ah, when will the Gold Cock bring me pardon,
And I may return to you from banishment?

The Gold Cock was displayed as symbol for amnesty.

119. ON HEARING THE FLUTE IN THE YELLOW CRANE HOUSE

A wandering exile, I came away to Long Beach.
I gazed toward home, beyond the horizon,
Toward the city of Chang-an.
I heard some one in the Yellow Crane House,
Playing on the sweet bamboo flute
The tune of the "Falling Plum Flowers"...

It was May in the waterside City

120. ON HEARING THE FLUTE AT LO-CHENG ONE SPRING NIGHT

Whence comes this voice of the sweet bamboo,
Flying in the dark?
It flies with the spring wind,
Hovering over the city of Lo.
How memories of home come back to-night!
Hark! the plaintive tune of "Willow-breaking."...

The "Willow-breaking" was a popular parting song.

121. ON THE TUNG-TING LAKE—I

Westward from Tung-ting the Chu River branches out,
While the lake fades into the cloudless sky of the south.
The sun gone down, the autumn twilight steals afar over Chang-sha.
I wonder where sleep the lost queens of Hsiang of old.

These are two of the five poems Li Po composed at a boat party with Chia-chi and Li Hua while on his way to Yeh-lang. See the Introduction.
The Chu River. The Yangtze takes this name in this vicinity near the Tung-ting Lake, which comprises the ancient land of Chu.
The lost queens of Hsiang, i. e. O Huang and Hu Yin, the wives of Shun, who perished near the lake by the Hsiang River. See No. 92.

122. ON THE TUNG-TING LAKE—II

The autumn night is vaporless on the lake.
The swelling tide could bear us on to the sky.
Come, let us take the moonlight for our guide,
We'll sail away and drink where the white clouds are!

123. TO HIS WIFE

Divided from you, I lament alone under the skies of Yeh-lang.
In my moonlit house seldom a message arrives;
I watch the wild geese all go north in the spring.
And they come south—but not a letter from Yu-chang

This is evidently addressed to his last wife, who was staying at Yu-chang, in central Kiangsi, while Li Po was traveling westward to his place of banishment.

124. TO HIS FRIEND, WEI, THE GOOD GOVERNOR OF CHIANG-HSIA WRITTEN IN COMMEMORATION OF THE OLD FRIENDSHIP DURING THE DAYS OF HIS BANISHMENT AFTER THE TUMULT OF WAR.

Once I sought the City of White Jade in heaven,
The five palaces and twelve lofty towers,
Where gods of felicity stroked me on the forehead,
And I bound my hair and received the everlasting life.
Woe to me, I turned to the pleasures of the world,
Pondering deep on peace and war,
And the reigns of the ninety-six illustrious kings,
Whose empty fame hangs on the drifting vapor!
I could not forget the tumultuous battles;
Fain would I try the empire-builder's art
Of staking heaven and earth in one throw,
And win me the car and cap of the mandarin.
But time ordained a dire disappointment,
I threw my hopes and went, wandering wide.
I learned swordsmanship and laughed at myself.
I wielded my pen—what did I achieve after all?
A sword could not fight a thousand foemen;
The pen did steal fame from the four seas,
Yet it is a child's play not worth talking about,
Five times I sighed; and went out of the western metropolis.
At the time of my leaving
My hat-strings were wet with tears.
It was you, my friend, excellent and wise,
The peerless flower of our race,
Who spread the mat and drew the curtains round
For a parting feast to comfort me journeying far.
You came to see me off, you and your company on horseback,
As far as the Inn of Cavaliers.
There amid songs and tinkling bells,
Ere our hearts were sated,
The garish sun fell beyond the Kun-ming Lake.[10]
In October I arrived in the land of Yu Chow,
And saw the legions of star-beaming spears.
The northland by the sea, abandoned by our dear emperor,
And trusted to one like the monstrous whale,
That drinks up a hundred rivers at one draught,

---

[10]   This, the longest poem in the entire collection of Li Po's works, is in a way his autobiography. It was written after he was allowed to return from banishment in 759. See the *Introduction.*
     The first stanza tells of his early life of seclusion in the world of Taoistic visions; of his ambition; and of his disappointment at Chang-an, the western metropolis.
     The Inn of Cavaliers and the Kun-ming Lake are both situated in the vicinity of Chang-an. At the time of Li Po's departure from the capital (circa 745) Wei was evidently in Chang-an and was able to give him the big farewell demonstration described herein.

Was crumbling fast to utter ruin.
Knowing this, I could not speak out,
And vainly wished I had lived in the fabled isle without care.
I was like an archer who, cowed by the wolf,
Sets the arrow but dares not draw the bow-string.
At the Gold Pagoda I brushed my tears
And cried to heaven, lamenting King Chao.
There was none to prize the bones of a swift steed.
In vain the fleet Black Ears bounced lustily,
And futile it was, should another Yo-I appear.
I prodded on, a houseless exile—
All things went amiss;
I sped my horse and returned to your town.[11]
I met you and listened to your song and twanging strings,
Sitting ceremoniously in your flower-painted room.
Your prefecture alone possessed the peace of antiquity
And the balmy ease that lulled the mystical king Hsi to sleep.
You called for musicians, and the hall was gay:
Our banquet table laden with wine cups and jars,
And handsome files of men sitting with moth-eyebrowed girls,
Our feast went on in the light of blazing cressets.
Drunken, we danced amid the confusion of silken stools,
And round the rafters hovered our clear song—
So our revelry lasted till even after the dawn.
But you returned to Hsing-yang, your official days over.
What a multitude that gathered for the farewell rites,
And those tents erected on the roadside near and far!
Once parted, we were divided by a thousand miles,
With our fortunes differing like summer and winter.

---

[11]   Yu Chow, the northland, is in the present Chili province. It was here that An Lu-shan was stationed with his star-gleaming legions, and Li Po detected the Tartar general's rebellious schemes, though he was obliged to keep silent. It was this region which comprised the state of Yen in the 4th century B. C. and where King Chao ruled and built the Gold Pagoda.

King Chao once questioned his retainer, Kuo Wei, as to the ways of attracting the great men of the time to his court. Kuo Wei told his liege the following parable:

Once upon a time a certain king sent out his servant on a mission to secure a swift horse that could run a thousand li in a day. The servant returned with a bagful of bones of a horse which was said to have made a thousand li in a day. For these remains the servant had paid 500 pieces of gold. The king was angry, for he wanted a live horse. The servant replied, "When the world learns that your Majesty has spent 500 pieces of gold on a dead horse, the live ones will arrive without your looking for them." Indeed, three horses—all of them, one thousand li runners—arrived soon at the court.

"So my king," continued Kuo Wei, "if you really desire to show your high regard for men of great talent, begin with me who have but small talent!"

King Chao took the advice. He built the Gold Pagoda, and there he waited upon Kuo Wei as his teacher. Then many men of ability came from all parts of China to King Chao, and with their aid he became the most powerful of all kings.

The Black Ears was a famous swift horse.

Yo-I was one of those great men who came to King Chao. Li Po laments that now there is no sovereign seeking as earnestly as King Chao for men of talent. And these, of whom he is one, have no opportunity.

Summers and winters had come and gone—how many times?—
And suddenly the empire was wrecked.
The imperial army met the barbarian foe,
The dust of the battlefield darkened sky and sea,
And the sun and moon were no longer bright
While the wind of death shook the grass and trees.
And the white bones were piled up in hills—
Ah, what had they done—the innocent people?

The pass of Han-ku guarded the imperial seat of splendor,
And the fate of the empire hung on General Ku Shu.
He with his thirty thousand long-spear men
Surrendered, and opened the gate to the savage horde.
They tamed the courtiers like dogs and sheep,
And butchered the men who were loyal and true.
Both the sovereign and the heir fled from the palace,
And the twin imperial cities were laid to waste.[12]
The imperial prince, given the supreme command,
Held his armies in the stronghold of Chu;
But there was no discipline of Huan and Wen.
His generals herded bears and tigers in the ranks,
And men wavered in doubts and fears
While the rebellion raged like tempest.
You were defending Fang-ling, I remember,
With loyalty unsurpassed in all ages.

I lived then in the mountain of Incense Burner,
Eating the mist and washing my mouth in the crystal fountain.
The house door opened on the winding Nine Rivers,
And beneath my pillow lay the five lakes, one linked to another.
When the fleet came upstream in the midnight
And filled the city of Hsin-yang with flags and banners,
I, betrayed by my own empty name,
Was carried by force aboard the war-boat.
They gave me five hundred pieces of gold,
I brushed it away like a rack, and heeded not;
Spurned the gift and the proffered title—
For all that I was banished to the land of Yeh-lang.

Oh, the long road of a thousand miles to Yeh-lang!
The westward journey made me old.

---

[12]   Just in what prefecture Wei was stationed is not known. When his official term was over, he returned to Hsin-yang, a town on the west side of Chang-an. Sometimes the two names are applied synonymously to the capital.

The Chinese made a great deal of leave-taking, often erecting as in this case tents on the wayside and offering sacrifices to the god of the road for the safety of the one setting out on his journey.

These passages refer, of course, to the rebellion of An Lu-shan. General Ku Shu defended the Han-ku Pass, which is an older name for Tun Kuan. By the twin imperial cities the poet very probably means Hsing-yang and Chang-an, unless he means the latter and city of Lo-yang. See the *Introduction*.

Though the world was being put to order,
I was ignored like a stalk of frost-bitten grass.
The sun and the moon shine alike on all—
How could I complain of injustice to heaven?
You, good governor, adored like a god,
Took compassion on your old friend.
You invited me to be your guest of honor,
And we ascended three times the tower house of Yellow Crane.
I blushed to think of Mi Hsien, the poet-recluse—
How he would sit, looking complacently at the Parrot Isle.
No more heroes were born to the enchanted mountains of Fan.[13]
And the desolation of autumn covered the world.
But lo, the river swelling with the tides of Three Canyons,
And the thousands of junks that thronged these waters,
Jostling their white sails, gliding past to Yang-chow!
On looking out on these things, my grief melted away in my heart.

We sat by the gauze-curtained window that opened to the sky
And over the green trees that grew like hair by the waterside,
Watching the sun with fear lest it be swallowed by the mountains,
And merry at moonrise, drinking still more wine.

Those maids of Wu and pretty girls of Yueh,
How dainty their vermilioned faces!
They came up by the long flight of stairs; emerged,
From behind the bamboo screen, smiling;
And danced, silken-robed, in the wind of spring.

The host was reluctant to pause
Though the guests knelt and asked for rest.
You showed me your poem of Ching-shan,
Rivaling the native beauty of the lotus,
That rises from the lucent water, unadorned.

Your joyous spirit swelling over in your heart,
You called for me ever at your residence,
Your mansion whose red gate was guarded by men,
Holding their spears in stately rows.
Amid quaintly cut stones and trimmed bamboos
A rivulet ran, brimming with limpid water.
We went up and sat in the waterside pavilion,
And poured forth our souls in heroic discourses.

---

[13]   The imperial prince i. e. Li Ling, the Prince of Yung. See the *Introduction*.
    Li Po was quite willing to join the staff of the prince at the beginning; but when his rebellious intent became obvious, the poet retired to the mountain of Luh, near Kiu-kiang, or Hsin-yang, as it was called at the time. The Incense Burner is one of the peaks of the Luh mountain range.
    Wei was now the governor of Chiang-hsia, a district in southern Hupeh. The Yellow Crane House (See note, No. 40) looks over the Yangtze-kiang.

A word between us is precious like white jade,
And a pledge of ours more than yellow gold.
I was not unworthy of you, I venture to say,
And swore by the Blue Bird on my fidelity.

The happy magpie among the five-colored clouds
Came, flying and crying, from heaven.
The mandate of my pardon arrived, I was told,
And I could return from banishment in Yeh-lang.
It was as if warmth enlivened the frozen vale,
Or fire and flame sprang from the dead ashes.

Still the dogs of Chieh bark at Yao,
And the Tartar crew mock at the imperial command.
In the middle of the night I sigh four and five times,
Worrying ever over the great empire's affairs.
Still the war banners cover the sides of the two mountains,
Between which flows the Yellow River.
Our generals like frightened fowls dare not advance,
But linger on, watering their idle horses.
Ah, where shall we find a Hu-I, the archer,
Who with the first arrow will shoot down the evil star?[14]

POEMS BY OTHER POETS CONCERNING LI PO

PART II

The following poems by Tu Fu and others are but a few of many such collected by
Wang Chi and appended to his edition of Li Po's Complete Works. These poems are not
only beautiful in themselves but are of a peculiar interest in that they give a glimpse into
the charming circle of poets by whom Li Po was surrounded and esteemed so highly.

125. THE EIGHT IMMORTALS OF THE WINECUP

CHI-CHANG rides his horse, but reels
    As on a reeling ship.
Should he, blear-eyed, tumble into a well,
    He would lie in the bottom fast asleep.
Ju-yang PRINCE must have three jugfuls
    Ere he goes up to court.
How copiously his royal mouth waters
    As a brewer's cart passes by!
It's a pity, he mournfully admits,

---

[14]   Chieh is a notorious tyrant, and Yao a benign sovereign, of ancient China. By the "dogs of Chieh"
are meant Shih Ssu-ming and his cohorts, who kept up the rebellion started by An Lu-shan.
    Hu I, a famous archer of the legend, who shot down the false suns that appeared in the heavens and
devastated the crops. Here Li Po means a savior, who could deliver the empire from the clutch of the
rebels.

That he is not the lord of the Wine Spring.
Our MINISTER LI squanders at the rate
   Of ten thousand pence per day.
He inhales like a great whale,
   Gulping one hundred rivers;
And with a cup in his hand insists,
   He loves the *sage* and avoids the *wise.*
TSUNG-CHI, a handsome youth fastidious,
   Disdains the rabble,
And turns his gaze toward the blue heaven,
   Holding his beloved bowl—
Radiant is he like a tree of jade
   That stands against the breeze.
SU CHIN, the religious, cleanses his soul
   Before his painted Buddha,
But his long rites must needs be interrupted
   As oft he loves to go on a spree.
As for LI PO, give him a jugful,
   He will write one hundred poems.
He drowses in a wine shop
   On a city-street of Chang-an;
And though his sovereign calls
   Will not board the imperial barge.
"Please your Majesty," says he,
   "I am a god of wine."
CHANG HSU is a calligrapher of renown,
   Three cups makes him the master.
He throws off his cap, baring his pate
   Unceremoniously before princes,
And wields his inspired brush—lo!
   Wreaths of cloud roll on the paper,
CHAO SUI, another immortal, elate
   After full five jugfuls,
Is eloquent with heroic speech,
   The wonder of all the feasting hall.

                                           TU FU.

The Wine Spring, located in the western part of Kansu, is said to have possessed a natural fountain of wine.
The sage and the wise. See No. 126.

126. THE EX-MINISTER

Avoiding the *wise*, I've resigned
  From the empire's ministry.
Loving the *sage*, still I sip
  The soothing cup of wine.

Ah, those eager visitors of yesterday,
  Who flocked at the front of my gate—
How many of them have come
  This morning, I pray?

—LI SHIH-CHI

A book called "Facts about Poets" says: "In the latter part of the Kai-yuan Era (A. D. 713-742) the prime minister, Li Shih-chi, had an enviable reputation for his simplicity and rugged uprightness. Li Ling-fu hated him, and by slander and intrigue caused his retirement. All those at the court knew the innocence of Shih-chi, but the emperor neglected to consult him. Fretting under this mistreatment, Shih-chi drank wine daily and also made poems." Of which this is a specimen. He describes the solitude and ease of his private life.

By "avoiding the wise" is meant vacating one's official position in order to make way for the wise and talented. The phrase, first used by Shih Ching of the Han dynasty in his petition for his release from the office of the premier, had become a stock pretext for the retiring official. On the other hand, the thick wine was called the wise, *and the clear wine the* sage. *Hence, there is in this poem a play on words with a subtle irony, of a kind much relished by the literary Chinese.*

127. A VISIT TO FAN WITH LI PO

My honored friend, Li, writes excellent verses,
That ring at times like Ying-kao's masterly lines.
I, too, a sojourner of Tung Meng,
Love him as a younger brother loves the elder.
Drunk, we sleep both under one cover at night;
And in daytime we go together hand in hand.
Now longing for a place of quiet company,
We come to visit you on the city's northside.
Your little boy waits on us so handsomely,
Joy leaps in our hearts as we enter your gate.
What solitude! We hear only the chilly mallets,
And see the clouds bivouac before the old city wall.
Having always sung the ode of the sweet citron,
Who cares to seek for the soup of the water-herbs?
You desire not the debasement of official life,
But remain untrammeled like the blue, boundless sea.

TU FU.

This poem was written in the earlier days of their friendship when Li Po and Tu Fu were both in Shantung. Tung Meng is a district in that province.

128. PARTING WITH LI PO ON THE TUNG-TING LAKE

To-day at the time of falling leaves we meet only to part
On the autumn waters of the Tung-ting, that stretch afar to the horizon.
And while talking together of our good old time at the metropolis of gold,
We turn to the northern sky and gaze at the stars of the Ursa Major, our eyes filled with tears.

CHIA CHI.

The metropolis of gold is the capital of the empire, Chang-an, where both Li Po and Chia Chi had spent their more prosperous days.

129. AN INVITATION TO LI PO

In the cool autumn month—the Eight or the Ninth—
White is the dew, and desolate the garden arbor.

As I sat weary, devoid of the heart's buoyancy,
I heard the wind whisper to the leaves on the tree-top,
And longed to see some friend, a man of learning and valor,
With whom I could discourse over the past and the present,
When suddenly who should come but you, Honorable Li.

I greeted you with joy, regretting only it had not been sooner.
I clapped my hands at your enchanting utterances;
We talked metaphysics; we bubbled with laughter.
You expounded the vicissitudes of the past dynasties,
And made visible the exploits of kings and conquerors.

A knap-sack on your back, filled with books,
You go a thousand miles and more, a pilgrim.
Under your sleeve there is a dagger,
And in your pocket a collection of poems.
Your eyes shine like luminous orbs of heaven
When you recite your incomparable songs and odes.
You sip wine and twang your lute strings
When the winter's breath congeals the crystaline frost.

To-day I laid bare before you
All things long stored in my heart.
Now my family has a villa,
Situated on the north side of Mount Sung.

One sees the bright moon rise over the peak,
And the chaste beams silver the transparent stream.
The clouds scatter, and the house is quiet;
The passing wind bears the aroma of pine and cassia.
If you will deign to make a visit thither with me,
I will not forget the honor for a thousand years.

TSUI TSUNG-CHI.

Tsui Tsung-chi, the handsome man and the fourth of the Immortals in Tu Fu's poem. He was a good friend of Li Po, and there are a number of poems extant, that were written by the latter to him. See the Introduction.

Mount Sung, one of the five sacred mountains, is to the southeast of Honan-fu, Honan.

130. TO LI PO ON A SPRING DAY

Po, the poet unrivaled,
in fancy's realm you soar alone.
Yours is the delicacy of Yui,
And Pao's rare virility.
Now on the north of the Wei River
I see the trees under the vernal sky
While you wander beneath the sunset clouds
Far down in Chiang-tung.
When shall we by a cask of wine once more
Argue minutely on versification?

TU FU.

Yui and Pao refer respectively to Yui Hsin and Pao Chao, both noted poets of the 6th century.

131. TO LI PO

Long have I not seen you, Li.
Poor man, for your feigned madness
The world would have you die.
But my heart dotes on your gifted soul
For the thousand poems of your nimble wit,
For the one wine-cup—your penury's balm.
So to your place of reading in Mount Kuang
Come back, O white-headed one! It is time.

TU FU.

Written possibly after the incarceration of Li Po at Kiu-kiang and while the death sentence was hanging over his white head.

132. THE GRAVE OF LI PO

By the River of Tsai-shih
There is Li Po's mound
Amid the endless plains of grass
That stretch to the cloud-patched sky.
Alas! here under the fallow field
The bones of him lie whose writing once
Startled heavens and shook the earth.
Of all poets, unfortunate as they be,
There is none wretcheder, Master, than you.

PO CHU-I.

It is likely that Po Chu-I visited the grave of Li Po during his banishment at Kiu-kiang, 815-818.

BIOGRAPHICAL NOTES ON LI PO BY CHINESE AUTHORS

PART III

The following translations are offered as much because of their contents as because of the interest they possess as types of ancient Chinese writing at and about Li Po's time.

Li Yang-ping's Preface is written in the euphuism of the Six Dynasty Period with its parallel constructions, profuse classical allusions, and curious hyperboles. Though the author's judgment is not worth any serious consideration, this is the first critical essay on Li Po.

The two biographies from the "Books of Tang," in spite of their brevity and mistakes, remain still the official and only extant authentic accounts of the poet's life written in Chinese.

THE PREFACE TO THE FIRST EDITION OF THE POETIC WORKS OF LI TAI-PO

By LI YANG-PING[15]

MAGISTRATE OF TANG-TU, HSUAN-CHOU, OF THE TANG DYNASTY

Li Po, surnamed Tai-po, was a man of Cheng-chi of Lunghsi and a descendant in the ninth generation from Kao, who was the king Wu-chao of the Liang state.

His early ancestors, one after another, wearing the gem and girdle,[16] were possessed of preeimence and renown. Later one Li, though he had done no wrong, was exiled and dwelt in the land of Chiao-chi, where he changed his names. The five generations from Chiung-shan to the emperor Shun were in the peasantry; and so were the Li's, and they did not shine greatly. Which is a thing to be lamented.

---

[15] Li Yang-ping, Li Po's kinsman, and a calligrapher of note, brought out the poet's works in 762.
[16] "Wearing gem and girdle" implies holding governmental office.

No. 113. THE SONG OF LUH SHAN.

> Edkins, *On Li Tai-Po*. Song of Lushan.
> Florenz, *Gedichte v. Li Taipe*. Lied auf dem Lushan.

No. 114, 115, 116. TO HIS WIFE ON HIS DEPARTURE.

> Lowell, *Fir-Flower Tablets*. Separated by Imperial Summons from Her who Lives Within.

No. 117. ON HIS WHITE HAIR.

> Giles, *Hist. of Chinese Lit.* P. 153.
> —, *Chinese Poetry in Eng.* Within a Mirror.
> Oehler-Heimerdinger, *Chinesische Lyric.* Wenn All mein Weisses Haar.

No. 118. TO THE HONORABLE JUSTICE HSIN.

No. 119. ON HEARING THE FLUTE IN THE YELLOW CRANE HOUSE.

No. 120. ON HEARING THE FLUTE IN LO-CHENG ONE SPRING NIGHT.

> Lowell, *Fir-Flower Tablets*. Hearing a Bamboo Flute on a Spring Night in the City of Lo Yang.

No. 121, 122. ON THE TUNG-TING LAKE, I, II.

No. 123. TO HIS WIFE.

No. 124. TO HIS FRIEND WEI, THE GOOD GOVERNOR OF CHIANG-HSIA. WRITTEN IN COMMEMORATION OF THE OLD FRIENDSHIP DURING THE DAYS OF HIS BANISHMENT AFTER THE TUMULT OF WAR.

———

No attempt was made to list previous translations for the following poems in Part II.

No. 125. THE EIGHT IMMORTALS OF THE WINE-CUP.
TU FU.

No. 126. THE EX-MINISTER OF STATE.
LI SHIH-CHI.

No. 127. A VISIT TO FAN WITH LI PO.
TU FU.

No. 128. PARTING WITH LI PO ON THE TUNG-TING LAKE.
CHIA CHI.

82

In the beginning of the Shen-lung era[17] the family escaped and returned to Shuh. Our "Po-yang"[18] was born, pointing to the plum tree. On the evening of his birth his mother dreamed of the planet of Chang-keng. So when the babe was born, he was named Po, and surnamed Tai-po. They said he was begotten by the spirit of the Great White Star.

He would read nought but the books of the sages and was ashamed to write after the lewd school of Chen and Wei.[19] Thus, his words resembled the speech of the heavenly genii. His writing consists of many satires and allegories.

From the ages of the Three Dynasties[20] and the times of the *Feng* and *Sao*,[21] there has been but one man, our master, who could run the race with Chu and Sung, and who could whip and spur Yang and Ma.[22] Yea, our master walks alone in the history of a thousand years. Is it any wonder that he swayed princes and earls who hurried to him, arraying their multitudinous arms and linking the cross-bars of their carriages while numerous men of wisdom gathered to do homage as the birds flock to the Phoenix?

The Lord of the Yellow Gate[23] says that it is the Censor of the Court, Chen,[24] who stayed the tide of decadence and wrought a change of literature in form and matter. But even under our present dynasty the poesy was infected with the manners of the seraglio school of the Liang and Cheng dynasties[25] until our master swept them and banished them from the earth, causing a marvelous change. Now the books of poesy, new or old, are cast off and do not prevail. But the writings of our master cover the universe. He in his power may be said to rival Nature, the creator and transformer.

In the beginning of the Tien-pao era[26] his Majesty's grandsire deigned to summon him. At the Gate of Gold Horse the emperor alighted from his car and walked to meet our master, welcoming him as though he were the venerable Chi the Hoary;[27] granted him a feast on the table of seven jewels and made him eat, seasoning the soup for him with his august hands. He said: "Thou art a cotton-clothed one, but art become known to me. How could this have been but that thou hast cherished virtue and righteousness?" So the Emperor let him sit in the Hall of Gold Bells, and go in and out of the Han-ling Academy; and questioned him on the affairs of government and privily ordered him to compose mandates and rescripts. Of this none was aware.

But when the true and the base are put side by side, the gifted one is injured and slanders are made, while the candid word of virtue fails. The emperor neglected him. Our

---

[17] The Shen-lung era covers the years 705 and 706. The statement here is obviously a mistake since by this time Li Po was already a boy of four or five. The New Book of Tang incorporates this mistake.

[18] Po Yang. The surname of Laotzu, the founder of Taoism, who was born in 604 B. C. miraculously from the left side of the mother. And at his birth he pointed to a plum tree. Here Li Yang-ping alludes to Li Po metaphorically.

[19] Chen and Wei are the names of states under the Chou dynasty, which contributed love songs to the Book of "Odes" compiled by Confucius.

[20] The Three Dynasties. The Hsia, the Shang and the Chou, comprising the years 2205-255 B. C.

[21] Feng and Sao are styles of ancient poetry. The Feng is found in the Confucian "Odes" while the Sao originated with Chu and Sung (i. e. Chu Yuan and Sung Yu) of the 4th and 3rd centuries B. C.

[22] Yang and Ma. Yang Hsiung (53 B. C.—A. D. 18) and Ssuma Hsiang-ju (died 117 B.C.), two noted poets of the Han Dynasty.

[23] The Lord of Yellow Gate. Refers to a certain Lu, a successful statesman as well as a gentleman of parts.

[24] Censor of the Court, Chen. Chen Tsu-ang, a poet and an intimate friend of Lu above.

[25] The Liang and Chen dynasties covered respectively A. D. 502-556 and 557-587, preceding the Tang dynasty.

[26] The Tien-Pao era covers the years 742-755.

[27] Chi, the Hoary. Refers to Chi Li-chi, one of the so-called "Four Gray-heads," of the 3rd century B. C. who withdrew from the world toward the close of the reign of the First Emperor of the Chin dynasty, but who reappeared upon the establishment of the Han dynasty and were welcomed and venerated by the new emperor.

master drank wine and by his indulgence obscured himself. And when he made poems and songs, he spoke often of the East Mountain. With Ho Chi-chang, Tsui Tsung-chi and the rest, he did also the revel of the Eight Immortals. Chi-chang called him "a god in exile." So his comrades at the court made compositions, entitled "The Song of the God in Exile," which were several hundred in number, and most of which mentioned our master's disappointments in life. The Son of Heaven, knowing that he could not be retained, gave gold and let him depart.

Thereafter he went with Yen-yun, visiting-inspector of Chen-liu,[28] to the High Heavenly Priest of Pe-hai, whom he petitioned and was bestowed the Taoist tablet at the Purple Peak Temple in Chi-chou.[29] He only desired to return east to Peng-lai[30] and ride with the *winged man* to the Scarlet Hill of immortality.

I, Yang-ping, was then trying my harp-playing and singing[31] at Tang-tu, although it was not what my heart coveted. Our master, forsaking me not, took a skiff and came to see me. It was when I was about to hang up my mandarin cap[32] that our master sickened. His manuscripts in ten thousand bundles and his hand collections were not yet arranged. So while lying on his pillow, he delivered them to me to be put in order. In discoursing on the significations of the *Kuan-chu*, now I feel ashamed to Pu Shang;[33] while in expounding the words of the *Spring* and *Autumn* I must forever blush before Tu Yu.

Since confusion befell the mid imperial plains,[34] our master sought refuge elsewhere for eight years. His writings of those years were lost, nine out of ten. What are preserved herein, are for the most part what I obtained from others.

Done on the I-chiu, the 11th moon of the First Year of the Pao-ying Era. (762).

LI PO—A BIOGRAPHY BY LIU HSU

(From the "Old Book of Tang"[35])

Li Po, surnamed Tai-po, was a man of Shantung.[36] While young, he possessed a superior talent, a great and taneless spirit, and fantastical ways of transcendent mind. His father was Captain of Jen-cheng, and there Po made his home. While young still, he with the youths of Luh—Kung Chao-fu, Han Chun, Pei-Cheng, Chang Shu-ming, and Tao-

---

[28] Chen-liu. A city near Kaifeng-fu, Honan.

[29] Chi-chou. The present city, Chinan-fu, Shantung.

[30] Peng-lai is a fabled island in the eastern sea; and the Scarlet Hill a dwelling place of exalted spirits. The Winged Men are those who have attained the highest rank in the Taoist Orders.

[31] To do "harp-playing and singing" means simply to govern, the phrase having a classic allusion to the story of the legendary emperor Shun of whom it is written, "Shun sang the Song of the South Wind, and there was peace in the land." Here the writer simply means that he, Yang-ping, was governor of Tang-tu. The Preface by Li Yang-ping.

[32] To "hang up one's mandarin cap" is to resign from office. Yang-ping was transferred from Tang-tu to Chin-yun Chekiang, in 763.

[33] Pu-shang (born, 507 B. C.), a disciple of Confucius, had the distinction of being entrusted by his master with the famous collection of Odes, the "Shi King," of which Kuan-chu forms a part. Tu Yu of the 3rd century, A. D., was a celebrated commentator on another Confucian classic, the *Spring and Autumn*. By his metaphorical allusions to these eminent men and books Li Yang-ping means to exalt the works of Li Po which he is editing and commenting upon.

[34] The "Confusion," of the "mid imperial plains" refers to the Rebellion of An Lu-shan which was started in 755.

[35] Li Hsu (897-947) wrote the "Old Book of Tang," a chronicle of the Tang dynasty, with a large number of biographies. The book was completed in 934.

[36] Li Po was not born in Shantung, but made his home there for a time as is told in the Introduction. Jen-cheng is a city in Shantung.

Mien—retired in the mountain of Chu-lai, where they drank wine freely amid blithe singing. They were known at the time as "the Six Idlers of the Bamboo Valley."

Early in the Tien-pao era Po went traveling to Kuei-chi. He retired to a district in Yen with a Taoist, whose name was Wu-yun. Yun was called and went up to the imperial palace. He recommended Po to the court. And they were both ordered to wait upon the emperor in the Han-ling Academy.

Po loved wine as hithertofore; and with his drinking companions drowsed daily in the tavern.

The emperor Hsuan Tsung arranged tunes and desired to have new words for the court music. At once he summoned Po from the Tavern where he lay. Men took water and dashed it on his face, after which he was made to hold the writing brush. Anon, he composed ten or more songs. The emperor was much pleased withal.

Once while dead drunk in the palace hall Po held out his feet and made Kao Li-shih to pull off his shoes. Because of this he was dismissed and sent away.

Now he wandered over lakes and rivers. He drank heavily all day long. At this time Tsui Tsung-chi, the Court Historian, demoted, was serving at Chin-ling. With Po he matched poems and drank wine. One moonlight night they took a boat from Tsai-shih to Chin-ling. Arrayed in the palace robe of brocade, Po sat in the boat, laughed and rolled his intrepid eyes as though there were no mortals near him. Ere this, Ho Chi-chang met Po and praised him, saying, "This man is a god exiled from the heaven above."

In the rebellion of Luh-shan the emperor Hsuan Tsung made his progress to the land of Shuh. On his way he appointed Ling, Prince of Yung, as supreme Military Commander of Chiang and Hwai Regions and Governor-general of Yang-chou. Po was at Hsuan-Chou, and had an audience of the prince, and at last entered his service. Prince of Yung plotted conspiracy, and was defeated in the war. Po, involved, was sentenced to perpetual banishment to Yeh-lang. Later he was pardoned and enabled to return. He died at last at Hsuan-cheng with too much drinking. There are twenty volumes of his writing which prevail at this time.

LI PO—A BIOGRAPHY by SUNG CHI

(From the "New Book of Tang"[37])

Li Po, surnamed Tai-po, is a descendant in the ninth generation from the emperor Hsing-sheng. His ancestor in the latter part of the Sui dynasty was for some wrong-doing exiled to the west barbarian land; but the family escaped and returned in the beginning of the Shen-lung era. They sojourned in Pa-hsi.

At the time of Po's birth his mother dreamed of the planet of Chang-keng, and because of this he was named after the star. At ten years of age he was versed in "the Odes" and "the History." When he was grown up, he hid himself in the Min Mountain, and would not respond though the province called for men of talent.

Su Ting became Governor of I-chou. On seeing Po, he wondered and said: "This lad is a genius, he is brilliant and singular. If a little more learning be added, he may be compared with Hsiang-ju." But Po delighted in strategems of crisscross alliances, took to swordsmanship, and to errantry, scorning riches but esteeming alms-giving.

---

[37]The "New Book of Tang" was finished in 1060 by Ou-yang Hsiu and Sung Chi. Sung Chi, who did all the biographies in this book died in 1061.

Later he sojourned in Jen-cheng; and with Kung Chao-fu, Han Chun, Pei Cheng, Chang Shu-ming, and Tao-mien, dwelt in the Chu-lai Mountain, daily drinking till they sank to the ground. They called themselves, "the Six Idlers of the Bamboo Valley."

At the beginning of the Tien-pao era he journeyed south to Kuei-chi, where he made a friend of Wu-Yun. Yun was summoned to court. So arrived Po also at Chang-an. He went to see Ho Chi-chang. Chi-chang saw his writing and said with a sigh, "You are a god in exile." He spoke to the emperor Hsan Tsung. Po was given audience in the Hall of Golden Bells; he discoursed upon the affairs of the world, and presented an ode. The emperor made him eat, seasoning the soup for him. A rescript was issued, by which Po was appointed to serve in the Han-ling Academy.

Po still went with his drinking companions, and drowsed in the market place.

The emperor sat in the Pavilion of Aloes. Stirred by a fancy, he desired to obtain Po to write songs to music. Po was summoned in, and he was drunk. The attendants took water and washed his face. When he recovered somewhat, he was handed a writing brush, and made compositions. Exquisite and graceful and finely finished they were, yet he made them without stopping to think. The emperor liked Po's talent, and often banqueted with him.

Once while attending upon the emperor, Po grew drunk and made Kao Li-shih pull off his shoes for him. Li-shih, a favorite of the throne, was humiliated thereby. He pointed out to Yang Kuei-fei a poem of Po, and caused her wrath. So when the emperor desired to appoint Po to office, then she stopped him.

Po himself, knowing he could not be taken in by those near the throne, all the more abandoned himself to recklessness. With Ho Chi-chang, Li Shih-chi, Chin, Prince of Ju-nan, Tsui Tsung-chi, Su Chin, Chang-Hsu, and Chiao Sui, he made up the "Eight Immortals of the Wine-cup." He implored for permission to return to the mountains; and the emperor gave gold and let him go.

Po roamed hither and thither. One time he took a boat with Tsui Tsung-chi from Tsai-shih to Chin-ling. Arrayed in the palace robe of brocade, he sat in the boat as though there were no mortal near him.

At the time of Au Lu-shan's rebellion Po lingered between the Su-sung and the Kuang-luh mountains. Ling, Prince of Yung, called him and made him a subordinate of his staff. When Ling started war, Po fled to Peng-tse. But with the fall of Ling, Po was sentenced to death. Ere this, when Po was stopping in Ping-chou, he met Kuo Tsu-i and admired him. Once Tsu-i broke the law, and Po came to rescue and had him freed. So now Tsu-i petitioned to ransom Po with his own rank and title whereupon a rescript was issued for his perpetual banishment at Yeh-lang.

He received pardon, and returned to Hsin-yang. There he was imprisoned on account of a certain affair,[38] when Sung Jo-ssu on his way to Honan with his army of three thousand men of Wu came to Hsin-yang, released the prisoner, and placed Po on his general staff. But before long he resigned. When Li Yang-ping became Governor of Tang-tu, Po went to live with him.

Emperor Tai Tsung ascended the throne,[39] and he summoned Po to take the office of the censor of the court; but Po was then dead. His years were sixty and a little more.

In his old age Po was fond of Taoism. He crossed the Bull Rock Shoal and reached

---

[38] This story of Li Po's second incarceration and his subsequent relations with Sung Jo-ssu is not authentic. Sung Jo-ssu was the man who memorialized the throne on behalf of Li Po at the occasion of the latter's imprisonment.

[39] Tai Tsung ascended the throne in 763.

Ku-shu,[40] where the Green Hill of the House of Hsieh pleased him, and he wished to make it the place of his last rest. But when he died, he was buried at the East Base.

In the beginning of the Yuan-ho era[41] Fan Chuan-cheng, Inspector of Hsuan-she, performed rites at his grave, and forbade woodcutting at the place. He sought for descendants of his. There were only two granddaughters, who were married and were wives of peasants, but who carried with them an air of refinement. They wept and said, "Our grandfather wanted the Green Hill; but is buried at the East Base, that is not his true wish." Whereupon Chuan-cheng made a reburial and erected two monuments. He told the two women that he would marry them into the official class. They declined, saying, "It is our destiny to end in poverty and isolation. We desire not to re-marry." Chuan-cheng approved them, and relieved their husbands from the conscript labor for the state.

In the reign of the emperor Wen Tsung[42] by imperial edict Po in songs and odes, Pei-min in sword dance, and Chang Hsu in cursive calligraphy, were declared "the Three Paragons."

BIBLIOGRAPHY

NOTES ON THE CHINESE TEXTS

Very shortly after the death of Li Po, Li Yang-ping published a collection in ten books with a preface dated 762, in which he says that the poet had lost a large portion of the poems written during his wanderings after the Rebellion of An Lu-shan, and many pieces in the books had been obtained from friends. Under the Sung Dynasty and about the year 1000, Kuo Yo-shih brought out a collection of ten books, which he combined with that of Li Yang-ping, making twenty books with 765 poems altogether, beside ten books of miscellaneous writings. In 1064 the first two of the three volumes of another collection were discovered, adding 100 new poems. Wei Hao's collection in two books was not brought to light till 1068, which contributed 44 new pieces. Thus the collection grew. In 1080 Sung Ming-chiu published the complete works in thirty books, containing nearly 1000 poems and 66 pieces in prose. Under the Ming dynasty and in 1759 Wang Chi brought out the final edition of the complete works in 30 books, with copious annotations and six books of critical, biographical and miscellaneous matter gleaned and gathered from all possible sources. This edition was reprinted in 1908 by the Soo Yeh Company of Shanghai.

Besides those enumerated above, there have been published innumerable editions of complete works and selections in past centuries. I have used a modern Japanese edition of selected poems, consulted a Chinese edition of the Sung period in the Newberry Library of Chicago, and also the original Wang Chi edition of 1759 in the New York City Public Library. The textual variations are few and unimportant as far as the poems in the present book are concerned.

---

[40] Ku-shu. is not far from Tang-tu, which is an old name for Taiping, Anhwei.
[41] Yuan-ho era. 806-820.
[42] Wen Tsung reigned during 827-841.

TRANSLATIONS AND WORKS ON LI PO

The following books and periodicals are only the more important items of the Li Po Literature in English, French, and German, which have come to the writer's notice. The figure in parenthesis at the end indicates the number of poems of Li Po translated in the book.

Joseph Marie Amiot. *Mémoires—concernant—l'Histoire; les Sciences, Les Arts, les Moeurs, les Usages, etc.—des Chinois, par les Missionaires de Pekin.* Paris, 1776-97. 14 vols. Contains a short biographical sketch, "Ly-pe, Poête." Vol. V., Pp. 396-399.

Anna Bernhardi. *Li Tai-Po. Mitteilungen des Seminar für Orientalische Sprädche,* die Königlishen Friedlich Wilhelms Universität, Berlin, 1916. Vol. 19, Pp. 105-138. Translations with the Chinese text. Introduction, notes, list of previous translations. Also a translation of Li Yang-ping's *Preface* with the original text. (41)

Hans Bethge. "Die Chinesische Flöte." Leipzig: Inselverlag, 1910. (15)

Charles Budd. "Chinese Poems." Oxford: Oxford University Press, 1912. A discussion of Chinese versification in the Introduction. Translations in rhymed verse. (1)

L. Cranmer-Byng. "A Lute of Jade." London: J.

Murray, 1911. New York: E. P. Dutton & Co., 1918. Poems of different periods. The Introduction covers "the Poets of the Tang Dynasty" and "a Poet's Emperor" (Hsuan Tsung). (8)

— —"A Feast of Lanterns." London: J. Murray, 1916. New York: E. P. Dutton & Co., 1918. (6)

Joseph Edkins. "On Li Tai Po." *Journal of the Pekin Oriental Society,* 1890. Vol. II., No. 5, Pp. 317-364. A paper read before the society on December 21, 1888. Translations in rhymed verse with Chinese text. (24)

Karl Florenz. "Gedichte von Li Taipe" in "Beitrage für Chinesische Poesie." *Mitteilungen der Deutschen Geselschaft für Natur—und Völkerkunde Ostasiens,* 1889. Vol. I, Pp. 44-61. Contains a biography, notes and the original Chinese text. (12)

A. Forke. "Blüthen Chinesischer Dichtung." Magdburg, 1899. Poems of the Han, the Six Dynasties, as well as the Tang periods, done in rhymed verse. Illustrations. (39)

Judith Gautier. "Poéms Chinois de Tous les Temps." Revue de Paris, June, 1901. (3)

— —"Le Livre de Jade." Paris, 1867 and 1918.

— —"Chinese Lyrics." From "The Book of Jade" translated by James Whithall. New York: B. W. Huebsch, 1918. (9)

H. A. Giles. "Gems of Chinese Literature." London: Bernard & Quaritch, 1884. (3)

—— "A History of Chinese Literature." London & New York: D. Appleton & Co., 1901. Pp. 151-156. (9)

—— "Chinese Poetry in English Verse." London: Bernard & Quaritch, 1898. A collection of Chinese poems from different periods, some of which are scattered throughout the "History of Chinese Literature" above. (21)

Wilhelm Grube. "Geschichte der Chinesischen Litterature." Leipzig: C. F. Amelangs Verlag, 1902. Pp. 277-284. (2)

Marquis d'Hervey Saint-Denys. "Poésie de l'Époque de Thang." Paris, 1862. An Anathology of the Tang period with notes. Biographical sketch of Li Po in the Introduction. (29)

Elizabeth Oehler-Heimerdinger. "Chinesische Lyric," Geist Ostens, München, 1913. I Jahrgang, Heft 3, Pp. 108-118.

Théodore Pavie. "Le Poète Ly Tai-pe." "Choix des Contes et Nouvelles." Paris, 1839. The story of Li Po, one of the *nouvelles*, is entirely unreliable, though not without elements of truth. Pp. 9-142.

Ezra Pound. "Cathay." London: Elkin Mathews, 1915. (11)

Franz Toussaint. "La Flute de Jade." Paris, 1920. A collection of very free and often fragmentary translations in prose. (17)

Arthur Waley. "Li Tai-Po." *The Asiatic Review*, London, October, 1919. Vol. XV, No. 44, Pp. 584-612. A paper which was read before the China Society. A valuable introduction with a translation of the poet's Biography in the "New Book of Tang." (24)

—— "More Translations from the Chinese." New York: Alfred Knopf, 1919. Poems of Li Po in this book are a selection from those in the *Asiatic Review*, above.

Florence Ayscough and Amy Lowell. "Fir-Flower Tablets." Boston: Houghton, Mifflin Co., 1921. Poems translated by Mrs. Ayscough and done into English verse by Miss Lowell. Mostly from Li Po and Tu Fu. (85)

For general reference a few more books may be suggested, though they do not particularly concern Li Po.

Demetrius C. Boulger. "The History of China." London: W. Thacker & Co., 1898.

Li Ung Bing. "Outlines of Chinese History." Shanghai: the Commercial Press, 1914.

Sir John Francis Davis. "Poeseos sinicae commentari" (the Poetry of China). London: Asher & Co., 1870.

Arthur Waley. "One Hundred and Seventy Chinese Poems." New York: Alfred Knopf, 1919.

Herbert Giles. "A Chinese Biographical Dictionary." London: B. Quaritch, 1892 and 1900.

POEMS OF LI PO TRANSLATED IN THIS BOOK

Previous translations, where they exist, are noted under each poem, although the compilation is by no means exhaustive. As for the full name of the translator and the title of his book or article, see the foregoing Bibliography.

No. 1. ON THE SHIP OF SPICE-WOOD.

>Pound, *Cathay*. The River Song.
>St. Denys, *Poésie*. En Bateau.
>Toussaint, *La Flute de Jade*. Le Bonheur.
>Waley, *Asiatic Rev*. River Song.
>Lowell, *Fir-Flower Tablets*. River Chant.

No. 2. IN THE MOUNTAINS ON A SUMMER DAY.

>Waley, *Asiatic Rev. and More Translations*.
>   In the Mountains on a Summer Day.

No. 3. NOCTURNE.

>Lowell, *Fir-Flower Tablets*. Autumn River Song.

No. 4. A FAREWELL SONG OF WHITE CLOUDS.

>Lowell, *Fir-Flower Tablets*. The Song of White Clouds.

No. 5. THE LONG DEPARTED LOVER.

>Bernhardi, *Li Tai-po*. In die Ferne.
>Toussaint, *La Flute de Jade*. La Chambre Vide.

No. 6, 7, 8 LADY YANG KUEI-FEI AT THE IMPERIAL FEAST OF THE PEONY, I, II, III.

Cranmer-Byng, *A Lute of Jade*. An Emperor's Love.
St. Denys, *Poésie*, Strophes Improvisées.
Toussaint, *La Flute de Jade*. Strophes Improvisées.
Lowell, *Fir-Flower Tablets*. Songs to the Peonies.

No. 9. A POEM COMPOSED AT THE IMPERIAL COMMAND IN THE SPRING GARDEN, WHILE LOOKING ON THE NEWLY GREEN WILLOWS BY THE DRAGON POND AND LISTENING TO THE HUNDRED-FOLD NOTES OF THE FIRST NIGHTINGALES.

No. 10. TO HIS FRIEND DEPARTING FOR SHUH.

Edkins, *On Li Tai-Po*. Address to a Friend.
Pound, *Cathay*. Leave-taking near Shuh.

No. 11. TO HIS THREE FRIENDS.

No. 12. ADDRESSED HUMOROUSLY TO TU FU.

No. 13. ON A PICTURE SCREEN.

No. 14. ON ASCENDING THE NORTH TOWER ONE AUTUMN DAY.

No. 15. THE SUMMIT TEMPLE.

No. 16. LAO-LAO TING, A TAVERN.

No. 17. THE NIGHT OF SORROW.

Edkins, *On Li Tai-Po*. Feeling Aggrieved.
Forke, *Blüthen Chin. Dicht*. Die Weinende.
Giles, *Gems of Chinese Lit*. Tears.
Lowell, *Fir-Flower Tablets*. Passionate Grief.

No. 18. THE SORROW OF THE JEWEL STAIRCASE.

Bethge, *Die Chin. Flöte*. Die Treppe im Mondlicht.
Edkins, *On Li Tai-Po*. Grief on Marble Steps.
Giles, *Gems of Chinese Lit*. From the Palace.
Pound, *Cathay*. The Jewel Stair's Grievance.
Toussaint, *La Flute de Jade*. Le Chagrin de Perron de Jade.

No. 19. THE GIRL OF PA.

Toussaint, *La Flute de Jade*. La Femme de Pa.

No. 20, 21, 22, 23, 24. THE WOMAN OF YUEH. I, II, III, IV, V.

Toussaint, *La Flute de Jade*. Les Jeunes Filles de Yueh. (No. 22)
Lowell, *Fir-Flower Tablets*. The Young Girls of Yueh. (No. 21, 22)

No. 25. THE SOLITUDE OF NIGHT.

Cranmer-Byng, *A Feast of Lanterns*. Along the Stream.
Edkins, *On Li Tai-Po*. Expressing What I Think.
Giles, *Chinese Poetry in Eng*. The Poet.
Waley, *Asiatic Rev. and More Translations*. Self Abandonment.

No. 26. THE MONUMENT OF TEARS.

No. 27. ON A QUIET NIGHT.

Bernhardi, *Li Tai-Po*. Gedanken in Stiller Nacht.
Cranmer-Byng, *A Lute of Jade*. Thoughts in a Tranquil Night.
Edkins, *On Li Tai-Po*. Thoughts on a Quiet Night.
Florenz, *Gedichte v. Li Taipe*. Gedanken in Stiller Nacht.
Forke, *Blüthen Chin. Dicht*. Mondenschein.
Bethge, *Die Chin. Flöte*. In der Fremde.
Giles, *Chinese Poetry in Eng*. Night Thoughts.
—, *Hist, of Chinese Lit*. P. 154.
St. Denys. *Poésie*. Pensee dans une Nuit Tranquille.
Toussaint, *La Flute de Jade*. Tristesse.
Lowell, *Fir-Flower Tablets*. Night Thoughts.

No. 28. THE BLUE WATER.

Bernhardi, *Li Tai-Po*. Die Weise von Grünen Wasser.
Edkins, *On Li Tai-Po*. Song of the Green Water.
Forke, *Blüthen Chin. Dicht*. Im Kahn.
Gautier, *Chinese Lyrics*. The Forbidden Flower.
Oehler-Heimerdinger, *Chinesche Lyric*. Im Kahn.

No. 29. THE CHING-TING MOUNTAIN.

Edkins, *On Li Tai-Po*. Sitting Alone on a Hill.
Florenz, *Gedichte v. Li Taipe*. Einsam auf dem Berge King-ting Sitzend.
Giles, *Chinese Poetry in Eng*. Companions.
—, *Hist, of Chinese Lit*. P. 154.

No. 30. WITH A MAN OF LEISURE.

> Florenz, *Gedichte v. Li Taipe*. Zechlage mit einem Einsiedler in Gebirge.
> Waley, *Asiatic Rev*. Drinking Together in the Mountains.

No. 31. THE YO-MEI MOUNTAIN MOON.

No. 32. ON THE CITY STREET.

No. 33. ON THE DEATH OF THE GOOD BREWER OF HSUAN-CHENG.

> Lowell, *Fir-Flower Tablets*. On the Subject of Old Tai's Wine-shop.

No. 34. TO HIS WIFE.

> Bernhardi, *Li Tai-Po*. Mein Frau.

No. 35. THE POET THINKS OF HIS OLD HOME.

> Edkins, *On Li Tai-Po*. East Mountain Recollected.

No. 36, 37. SORROW OF THE LONG GATE PALACE. I, II.

> Lowell, *Fir-Flower Tablets*. Bitter Jealousy in the Palace of the High Gate.

No. 38. AN ENCOUNTER IN THE FIELD.

> Lowell, *Fir-Flower Tablets*. A Poem Given to a Beautiful Woman Encountered
> on a Field-path.

No. 39. TO WANG LUN.

> Lowell, *Fir-Flower Tablets*. A Parting Gift to Wang Lun.

No. 40. ON SEEING OFF MENG HAO-JAN.

> Giles, *Chinese Poetry in Eng*. Gone.
> Pound, *Cathay*. Separation on the River Kiang.
> Lowell, *Fir-Flower Tablets*. At the Yellow Crane Tower, Taking Leave of Meng
> Hao-Jan on his Departure to Kuang Ling.

No. 41. ON BEING ASKED WHO HE IS.

No. 42. IN THE MOUNTAIN.

> Giles, *Hist, of Chinese Lit*. P. 155.
> Lowell, *Fir-Flower Tablets*. Reply to an Unrefined Person Encountered in the
> Hills.

No. 43. THE FAIR QUEEN OF WU.

Bethge, *Die Chin. Flöte*. Liebestrinken.
Gautier, *Rev. d. Paris*. Ivresse d'Amour.
—, *Chinese Lyrics*, Intoxication of Love.
Toussaint, *La Flute de Jade*. La Danseuse Un Peu Ivre.

No. 44. WHILE JOURNEYING.

Giles, *Chinese Poetry in Eng*. In Exile.

No. 45. THE RUIN OF THE KU-SU PALACE.

Toussaint, *La Flute de Jade*. Les Ruines de Sou-Tai.
Lowell, *Fir-Flower Tablets*. A Traveler Comes to the Old Terrace.

No. 46. THE RUIN OF THE CAPITAL OF YUEH.

No. 47. THE RIVER JOURNEY FROM WHITE KING CITY.

Edkins, *On Li Tai-Po*. From the City of White God.

No. 48, 49. BY THE GREAT WALL, I, II.

St. Denys, *Poésie*. Chansons des Frontières. (No. 48)
Toussaint, *La Flute de Jade*. Encore. (No. 48)
Lowell, *Fir-Flower Tablets*. Songs of the March, III. (No. 48)

No. 50. THE IMPERIAL CONCUBINE.

Bernhardi, *Li Tai-Po*. Acht Gedechte über die Freuden in Palastinnern.
Lowell, *Fir-Flower Tablets*. Pleasures within the Palace.
Giles, *Chinese Poetry in Eng*. A Favorite.
—, *Hist, of Chinese Lit*. P. 152.

No. 51. PARTING AT CHING-MEN.

No. 52. ON THE YO-YANG TOWER WITH HIS FRIEND CHIA.

No. 53. AWAKENING FROM SLEEP ON A SPRING DAY.

Bernhardi, *Li Tai-Po*. Der Trinke im Frühling.
Florenz, *Gedichte v. Li Taipe*. Lebensweisheit.
Forke, *Blüthen Chin. Dicht*. Im Rausch.
Giles, *Gems of Chinese Lit*. On Getting Drunk in Spring.
—, *Chinese Poetry in Eng*. The Best of Life is But—
St. Denys, *Poésie*. Un Jour de Printemps.

Toussaint, *La Flute de Jade*. Un Jour de Printemps.
Waley, *Asiatic Rev*. Waking from Drunkenness on a Spring Day.
Lowell, *Fir-Flower Tablets*. A Statement of Resolutions after Being Drunk on a Spring Day.

No. 54. THREE WITH THE MOON AND HIS SHADOW.

Bethge, *Die Chin. Flöte*. Drei Kameraden.
Florenz, *Gedichte v. Li Taipe*. Einsame Gelage im Monschein.
Giles, *Chinese Poetry in Eng*. Last Words.
—, *Hist, of Chinese Lit*. P. 153.
Grube, *Geschichte d. Chin. Lit*. Trinklieder.
Toussaint, *La Flute de Jade*. Petite Fête.
Waley, *Asiatic Rev. & More Translations*. Drinking Alone in the Moonlight, I.
Lowell, *Fir-Flower Tablets*. Drinking Alone in the Moonlight, I.

No. 55. AN EXHORTATION.

Bernhardi, *Li Tai-Po*. Afforderung zum Trinken.
Forke, *Blüthen Chin. Dicht*. Der Rabe.
St. Denys, *Poésie*. Chanson à Boire.
Waley, *Asiatic Rev*. Drinking Song.
Lowell, *Fir-Flower Tablets*. Drinking Song.

No. 56. THE INTRUDER.

Bernhardi, *Li Tai-Po*. Frühlings Gedanken.

No. 57. THE CROWS AT NIGHTFALL.

Bernhardi, *Li Tai-Po*. Des Rabens Nachtlicher Schrei.
Edkins, *On Li Tai-Po*. Raven Calling in the Night.
Forke, *Blüthen Chin. Dicht*. Der Rate.
Gautier, *Chinese Lyrics*. The Birds are Singing at Dusk.
Giles, *Hist. of Chinese Lit*. P. 155.
—, *Chinese Poetry in Eng*. For Her Husband.
Cranmer-Byng, *A Lute of Jade*. Memories with the Dusk Return.
Toussaint, *La Flute de Jade*. Les Corbeaux.

No. 58. TO MENG HAO-JAN.

No. 59. TO TUNG TSAO-CHIU.

Pound, *Cathay*. Exile's Letter.
Waley, *Asiatic Rev*. Sent to the Commissary, Yuan of Chiao City, In Memory of Former Excursions.

No. 60. TAKING LEAVE OF A FRIEND.

Forke, *Blüthen Chin. Dicht.* Geleit.
Gautier, *Rev. d. Paris.* Le Depart d'un Ami.
Giles, *Chinese Poetry in Eng.* A Farewell.
Pound, *Cathay.* Taking Leave of a Friend.
Lowell, *Fir-Flower Tablets.* Saying Goodbye to a Friend.

No. 61. MAID OF WU.

No. 62. THE LOTUS.

No. 63. TO HIS TWO CHILDREN.

No. 64. TO A FRIEND GOING HOME.

No. 65. A MOUNTAIN REVELRY.

No. 66. THE OLD DUST.

Giles, *Hist, of Chinese Lit.* P. 155.

No. 67. A PAIR OF SWALLOWS.

Toussaint, *La Flute de Jade.* La Fidélité.

No. 68. AT A RIVER TOWN.

No. 69. I AM A PEACH TREE.

No. 70. THE SILK SPINNER.

No. 71. CHUANG CHOU AND THE BUTTERFLY.

No. 72. THE POET MOURNS HIS JAPANESE FRIEND.

Edkins, *On Li Tai-Po.* A Japanese Lost at Sea.

No. 73. IN THE SPRING-TIME ON THE SOUTH SIDE OF THE YANGTZE KIANG.

No. 74. THE STEEP ROAD TO SHUH.

Waley, *Asiatic Rev.* The Ssuchuan Road.
Lowell, *Fir-Flower Tablets.* The Perils of the Shu Road.

No. 75. PARTING AT A TAVERN OF CHIN-LING.

Waley, *Asiatic Rev*. Parting with Friends at a Wine-shop in Chin-ling.
Lowell, *Fir-Flower Tablets*. The Poet is Detained in a Nanking Wine-shop on
the Eve of Starting on a Journey.

No. 76. THE PHOENIX BIRD TOWER.

Bernhardi, *Li Tai-Po*. Aufstieg auf dem Turme des Phoeniz-Paares in Chin-ling.
Pound, *Cathay*. The City of Cho-An.
Lowell, *Fir-Flower Tablets*. Feng Huang Tai.

No. 77. HIS DREAM OF THE SKY-LAND: A FAREWELL POEM.

Waley, *Asiatic Rev*. A Dream of Tien-Mu Mountain (a partial translation).

No. 78. IN MEMORIAM.

No. 79. ON THE ROAD OF AMBITION.

No. 80. TO TU FU FROM SAND HILL CITY.

Lowell, *Fir-Flower Tablets*. A Poem Sent to Tu Fu from Sha Chiu Cheng.

No. 81. A VINDICATION.

Waley, *Asiatic Rev. and More Translations*. Drinking Alone in the Moonlight,
III.
Lowell, *Fir-Flower Tablets*. Drinking Alone in the Moonlight, II.

No. 82. TO LUH, THE REGISTRAR.

No. 83. TO THE FISHERMAN.

No. 84. THE TEARS OF BANISHMENT.

No. 85. THE LOTUS GATHERER.

Bethge, *Die Chin. Flöte*. Am Ufer.
Cranmer-Byng, *A Lute of Jade*. On the Banks of Jo-yeh.
Gautier, *Chinese Lyrics*. At the River's Edge.
St. Denys, *Poésie*. Sur les Bords de Jo-Yeh.
Toussaint, *La Flute de Jade*. Sur les Bords de Jo-Yeh.
Waley, *Asiatic Rev*. On the Banks of Jo-Yeh.

No. 86. THE SPORT FELLOWS.

Forke, *Blüthen Chin. Dicht.* Die Kameraden.

No. 87. THE ROVER OF CHAO.

Forke, *Blüthen Chin. Dicht.* Der Fahrende Ritter.
Grube, *Geschichte d. Chin. Lit.* Ballade vom Fahrenden Ritter. P. 282.
St. Denys, *Poésie.* Le Brave.
Toussaint, *La Flute de Jade.* La Gloire.

No. 89. TO HIS FRIEND IN CHIANG-HSIA.

No. 90, 91. THE CATARACT OF LUH SHAN, I, II.

Florenz, *Gedichte v. Li Taipe.* Der Wasserfall am Lushan. (No. 90)

No. 92. BEREFT OF LOVE.

Waley, *Asiatic Rev.* The Distant Parting.

No. 93, 94. LADY WANG-CHAO, I, II.

Lowell, *Fir-Flower Tablets.* The Honorable Lady Chao. (No. 94)

No. 95. THE NORTH WIND.

No. 96. THE BORDERLAND MOON.

Bernhardi, *Li Tai-Po.* Der Mond über dem Kuan Berge.
Lowell, *Fir-Flower Tablets.* The Moon over the Mountain Pass.

No. 97. THE NEFARIOUS WAR.

Forke, *Blüthen Chin. Dicht.* Elend des Krieges.
Waley, *Asiatic Rev.* Fighting.
Lowell, *Fir-Flower Tablets.* Fighting to the South of the City.

No. 98. BEFORE THE CASK OF WINE.

Bernhardi, *Li Tai-Po.* Zwei Lieder beim Becher Wein.
Forke, *Blüthen Chin. Dicht.* Beim Wein.

No. 99. YUAN TAN-CHIU OF THE EAST MOUNTAIN.

Bernhardi, *Li Tai-Po.* Schreiben an Yuan Tan-Chiu.
Waley, *Asiatic Rev.* To Tan-chiu.

No. 100. LINES.

> Bernhardi, *Li Tai-Po*. Gedichte aus Zeilen von Drei, Fünf und Sieben Zeichen.
> Giles, *Chinese Poetry in Eng.* No Inspiration.
> Lowell, *Fir-Flower Tablets*. Word Pattern.

No. 101, 102, 103, 104. THE BALLADS OF THE FOUR SEASONS.

> Bernhardi, *Li Tai-Po*. Vier Wu Lieder nach Tsu-yeh Art.
> St. Denys, *Poésie*. Chanson des Quatre Saisons.
> Toussaint, *La Flute de Jade*. Chanson des Quatre Saisons.
> Cranmer-Byng, *A Lute of Jade*. Under the Moon. (No. 103)
> Giles, *Gems of Chinese Lit*. The Grass-Widow's Song. (No. 103)

No. 105, 106. TWO LETTERS FROM CHANG-KAN.

> Bernhardi, *Li Tai-Po*. Zwei Lieder aus Chang-Kan.
> Florenz, *Gedichte v. Li Taipe*. Das Lied von Chang-Kan. (No. 105)
> Pound, *Cathay*. The River Merchant's Wife: A Letter. (No. 105)
> Waley, *Asiatic Rev.* Chang-Kan. (No. 105)
> Lowell, *Fir-Flower Tablets*. Chang-Kan. (No. 105)

No. 107. ON ASCENDING THE SIN-PING TOWER.

> Florenz, *Gedichte v. Li Taipe*. Beim Aufsteigen im Hause, Sin-Ping-Lou.

No. 108. ON VISITING A TAOIST RECLUSE ON MOUNT TAI-TIEN, BUT FAILING TO MEET HIM.

> Florenz, *Gedichte v. Li Taipe*. Vergeblicher Besuch bei einem Einsiedler.
> Lowell, *Fir-Flower Tablets*. Visiting Taoist Priest on the Mountain that which Upholds Heaven; He is Absent.

No. 109. AT THE CELL OF AN ABSENT MOUNTAIN PRIEST.

> Florenz, *Gedichte v. Li Taipe*. Besuch bei einem Bergpriester, den Ich Nicht Antraf.

No. 110. ON A MOONLIGHT NIGHT.

> Florenz, *Gedichte v. Li Taipe*. Gedanken beim Betrachten des Mondes.
> Lowell, *Fir-Flower Tablets*. In Deep Thought, Gazing at the Moon.

No. 111. A VISIT TO YUAN TAN-CHIU IN THE MOUNTAINS.

No. 112. A MIDNIGHT FAREWELL.

THE END.